Empire 2.0

The following books by Régis Debray are available in English:

Revolution in the Revolution (1967)

The Border and a Young Man in the Know (1968)

The Chilean Revolution, Conversations with Allende (1971)

Prison Writings (1973)

Che's Guerrilla War (1974)

A Critique of Arms (1977)

Undesirable Alien (1978)

Teachers, Writers, Celebrities, the Intellectuals of Modern France (1981)

Critique of Political Reason (1983)

Charles de Gaulle, Futurist of the Nation (1994)

Media Manifestos (1996)

Against Venice (Anti-Voyages Series, No. 1, 1999)

Transmitting Culture (2000)

God: an Itinerary (2004)

Empire 2.0

A Modest Proposal
for a United States of the West
by Xavier de C***

Prologue by
Régis Debray

Translated by Joseph Rowe

THE TERRA NOVA SERIES
North Atlantic Books
Berkeley • California

Published by
North Atlantic Books
P.O. Box 12327
Berkeley, California 94712   Cover and book design by Paula Morrison

First published in France as *L'Édit de Caracalla,* Fayard, 2002.
Printed in the United States of America.
Distributed to the book trade by Publishers Group West.

Empire 2.0: A Modest Proposal for a United States of the West by Xavier de C*** is sponsored by the Society for the Study of Native Arts and Sciences, a nonprofit educational corporation whose goals are to develop an educational and crosscultural perspective linking various scientific, social, and artistic fields; to nurture a holistic view of arts, sciences, humanities, and healing; and to publish and distribute literature on the relationship of mind, body, and nature.

Library of Congress Cataloging-in-Publication Data
Debray, Régis.
    [Edit de Caracalla. English]
    Empire 2.0 : a modest proposal for a United States of the West / by Xavier de C*** ; by Régis Debray ; translated by Joseph Rowe.
        p. cm. — (The terra nova series)
    ISBN 1-55643-495-2 (pbk.)
    1. United States—Foreign relations—1989– 2. United States—Foreign relations—Europe. 3. Europe—Foreign relations—United States. 4. Anti-Americanism—Europe. 5. National characteristics, American. 6. National characteristics, European. 7. Imperialism. 8. Unilateral acts (International law) 9. Balance of power. 10. World politics—1989– I. Title: Empire two point zero. II. Title: Modest proposal for a United States of the West. III. Title. IV. Series.
    E895.D43 2004
    843'.914—dc22
                              2004006200

1 2 3 4 5 6 7 8 9 DATA 09 08 07 06 05 04

Introduction

What? Régis Debray, comrade-in-arms of Che Guevara, ex-guerilla against Empire, notorious anti-American, arguing that Europe should incorporate itself into an expanded U.S.A. called the United States of the West? That it should cheerfully embrace the Manifest Destiny of American empire by fighting small wars on distant frontiers, rebuilding oil pipelines, making the clocks run on time? Not exactly. This modest proposal (lucid, passionate, utterly perverse) is put forth in a letter from a fictional ex-schoolmate, high-level diplomat, and conservative alter ego, Xavier de C*** who explains to his old friend why he has chosen to become an American citizen in the wake of 9/11—why, in fact, it's time for Europe to bow to the realities of power and get with the program. ("'Those who are not with us are against us,' are the very pertinent words of my new President," writes de C to Debray. "And whether you like it or not, he's your new President too.")

Defenses of empire are a dime-a-dozen in this low, dishonest decade. None are as eerily convincing as Debray's breezy *faux*-defense in this part-epistolary novel, part-Borgesian fiction. Professor N..., a Straussian, actually contacted this publisher, North Atlantic Books, asking permission to publish excerpts of *Empire 2.0.* in a mainstream foreign policy magazine—he took it to be a feasible response to our "war with Islam" and the destined "clash of civilizations." True story. No doubt the irony-challenged professor had yellow-highlighted such sentences as "The West ... is a precarious island surrounded by seething hatreds" or "What better time than now, with the prairie crawling with hostile tribes, to begin putting all the wagons in a defensive circle?"

Fiction ensnares the Bad Reader. And not just here in the country of the literal. Some on the French Left thought Debray had argued the imperial case too well. He had lent his protagonist, Xavier de C***, too many of his own best qualities: wit, learning, concision, a taste for unpalatable truths, and—above all—the skilled, passionate oratory that has made him a leading spokesman of the eighteenth-century ideal of the secular and egalitarian Republic. Where does Debray really stand? they wondered aloud.

Where he always has. Where he stood with Che and Allende. Against empire. Those unsure of this should check out his *New York Times* op-ed of February 23, 2003. Speaking against the imminent invasion of Iraq, he rejects America's "impatient Divine investiture." Europe, he says, has learned "to distinguish politics from religion," while America, hostage to "an altogether Biblical self-assurance," sees itself as "the predestined repository of Good, with a mission to strike down Evil." By invading an Arab country, "Osama bin Laden's fondest wish," America will only pump up an "ebbing fundamentalism" and expose itself to a law of unintended consequences unknown, apparently, to its leaders. "Provoking chaos in the name of order," he adds, "and resentment instead of gratitude, is something to which all empires are accustomed. And thus it is that they coast, from military victory to victory, to their final decline."

Feel free then, fellow-traveler on the *Pequod,* to enjoy this bravura performance, and when you finish, let's head up on deck to take the harpoon out of the hands of our mad captain.

Philip Wohlstetter

Prologue

A man of quality went off to war, and never came home. From the other shore of America, he wrote to an old friend from university days, a mellowed Parisian with the perspective of distance. This letter arrived in the fall of the year 2001. The writer, a Frenchman by birth and education, had just become an American citizen. A high-level military intelligence advisor, a scholar whose passion is Classical Rome, and a man who has lived a life of action, he chose to write this letter in the world language of our time. There are some envelopes you wish you hadn't opened. Their content is brutal and painful. Nevertheless, when some time has passed, you wonder if this might be one of those pains that are salutary. I ask of the reader only to continue all the way to the end of this book, without becoming discouraged.

R. D.

Washington, D.C., October 10, 2001

My old friend Debray,

The past is over. You can guess which past I mean, since I'm no longer writing you in our common lingo. But don't think this indicates any spiteful feelings toward my diminutive country of birth, still less a gush of emotion, or some sort of swagger. I had two or three acquaintances who were killed in the attacks on the World Trade Center, but strangely, no one I knew at the Pentagon was harmed, and God knows I've spent a lot of time there over the years. But I shall not indulge in anger or emotionalism. Régis, my friend, you know me well enough to know that I am anything but a hothead. For years, I have desired this change of citizenship—and without resorting to the notorious marriage of convenience. I wanted to go through the ritual the authentic way, without using any of my connections, just like any other conscientious immigrant. You'll be glad to know I breezed through all the tests of language and history, and never breathed a word to my former colleagues at the French embassy. So there it is. No more green card, and a new passport.

You should have seen me swearing the oath of allegiance at the Immigration office that gloomy September morning in New York, with people wandering through streets still grey from the ashes, and lingering odors of burnt rubber and melted wiring. Standing before the Stars and Stripes, hand on my heart! Not many candidates were there that morning, but some of the employees had tears in their eyes, proud of themselves and of us. They even congratulated us for our "act of courage in a dark time like this." There were only three of us, and it was like a family reunion: one Italian, one Dutchman, and one Gaul, yours truly. Not a single Asian or Latino. All Europeans. Chance had arranged things well that day.

A good sign, I thought. While pledging allegiance, I had the feeling of fulfilling some *agenda dei*.[1] Far from renouncing my millennial European heritage, I felt that I was consummating it, by affirming the only possible future it really has. But before you begin hurling accusations at me (defeatist, mercenary, turncoat, etc.), please bear me out and hear my reasons. You are the first Frenchman of France to be let in on the secret. Isn't that odd? For me to choose you of all people as confidant, a staunch "anti-American." (I use the quotation marks because you stand much higher in

---

[1] "Plan of God." [All footnotes are by the editor/translator, unless marked by the initials R.D. All footnote translations in quotes are from Latin, unless noted otherwise.]

my esteem than your naughty reputation). To choose as witness my oldest friend from the opposite political camp—this gesture forces me to take a clear and sober look at myself. And in choosing you as the target of my reflections, I am perhaps also addressing my own former self. You know, ever since our school days, I never entirely gave up on winning you over. You're certainly not an anti-Semite, so why be anti-American? Both are viruses of the same strain, the Bolshevik disease. It's not capitalism the French Left is fighting, it's democracy. What it really opposes is the creative freedom of money, of conscience, and of voting. The socialism of resentment! It's time you broke free of it. Granted, it's not always easy to be in tune with the times—but since September 11, some of those old leftist clichés are wearing pretty thin, don't you think?

"And our civilization, like all the others"—sure, we all know that line, we used to quote and recite it all the time—"is also mortal." But that didn't prepare us for *seeing* it with our own eyes. Those video clips played over and over must have brought it home to you too, just how fragile our Eternal City really is. The world we no longer dare call the free one is no more invulnerable than a Tower of Babel reaching up toward the sun. Bin Laden made the poet Valéry's phrase clear even to illiterates: "You have had the words. Now here is the image." Scourge from the skies, or hand of God?

May the hammer-blow that struck the Twin Towers (our own Pillars of Hercules, like the double bars on the dollar sign) resound in your ears like a giant bell. Perhaps it was not a superiority complex (let us hope not), but a kind of heedless laziness, a soft and self-indulgent feeling of achievement, which prevented the West from realizing that it is a precarious island, surrounded by seething hatreds. It is here that we run up against a wall, faced with our secret contradictions. With all the current talk of cultures in conflict, we have been overlooking the shock of our own culture confronting itself: our cowardice, our routines, our lullabies. The euphoria of a self-absorbed leadership is responsible for this, and it will not survive this wake-up call, an alarm bell that is ringing just as loudly for you Europeans. Berlusconi committed the diplomatic sin of saying in public what most think in private: sorry, but our civilization *is* superior to that of Islam. With regard to amenities, respect for human rights (especially those of women), freedom of intellectual inquiry, and scientific progress, who can say the contrary? (Though I grant you, there are some things that should not be said.) No, let us not succumb to the arrogance of *Il Cavaliere*[2]— above all, let us be more practical. Let us begin by saving the house from the brewing storm, and in such a way that it will

---

[2] Italian nickname for Berlusconi.

6

still be standing in a hundred years, this civilization of ours, alongside the others. The time is gone when one could speak of Civilization in the singular. We must face it: we Westerners represent only 15% of world population. And with globalization, we have become as conspicuous as a Dior show window in a Jakarta slum. An outlaw drives a car through the window, the alarms go off, but can the local police handle it? Don't count on it. In thirty years, there will be two billion Moslems. One human being in four will be labeled a "virtual terrorist." What are we to do? Well, we must change, or die. And who is this "we"? It's you and me. All us masses of Judeo-Christian-type folks who still enjoy the privilege of obeying the Ten Commandments when we feel like it, and dumping our leaders when the spirit moves us. Europe was divided against itself through most of the 20th century, and had to pass on the torch after two devastating wars fought on its soil. Aren't we now seeing the same suicidal impulses repeating themselves a century later, on a much bigger scale? Must the West, victim of its own shortsightedness, straining in all directions, come to an end, after a few illusory victories, by dissolving itself in surrender to the law of numbers? If we deserve the name of human beings, then we have no right to knuckle under to such a fate.

Fear has always been the great motivator. Challenge and response. It was only when the old nation-states of Europe teetered on the brink of the abyss after WWI, that the apostles of peace really saw the stupidity of nationalistic rivalries: European names such as Briand, Jouvenel, Coudenhove-Kalergi, Riou.... The idea of a pan-European union grew out of the First World Slaughter, and it took form after the second one, only to sink to the level of shopkeepers' haggling. After this latest electroshock treatment, may we also come to see the stupidity of Euro-American antagonism. The war against barbarism is the clarion call for a geopolitical vision, the only viable one from now on: a pan-Occidental union.

Has the whistling of mortar shells made me lose my mind? I've had my share of being shot at, with the Contras and the Mujahideen, and I assure you that no human missile—however inhuman—could make me lose my common sense. The effort we all must make is simply to raise ourselves to the level of the stakes. Those who are not content to passively watch events descend upon them, like snow on their TV screens, must strap on their seven-league boots, and leap across the chasm that separates their provincial little worlds from the planet, their tiny agendas from History. Chirac, Schroeder, Aznar, Berlusconi, and all those other tribal chieftains had better start to look beyond the next election and other local concerns. The curtain is closing on the clown show. The comfortable transatlanticism of nice intentions is dead. And with it has died the fantasy of isolationist America. A new chapter of history has opened. What is next?

"Not since Rome vanquished Carthage," one of my new compatriots has written, "has any other world power attained the heights where we now stand." Boastful, but true—yet only half-true. It sees the apple, but not the worm. The success of some, but not the resentment of others. The Capitol, but not the Tarpeian Rock. Still believing that it owned the world, it took September 11 for America to realize that it belongs to the world. "The 18th century was French, the 19th British, and the 20th American. The next century will also be American." As if History will serve up the same menu just for the asking! *Bis repetita placent?*[3] What naiveté, what myopia! No, the 21st century will be Western—perhaps, with a little luck—but only if we have the will to make it so. It will happen through a process of intellectual and moral transformation. It will be a mutation at the same level as the challenge facing us, and a radical break with all that governmental dead wood that still controls transatlantic relations between the two shores of *mare nostrum,*[4] relations that have become mired in the false security of "precedents."

---

[3] "Repetition gives pleasure."

[4] "Our sea," which meant the Mediterranean.

A civilization consists of a center and a periphery, at least in the reality established over centuries. Yet our editorialists seem to have no problem hawking wine from empty jugs. Their "Western World" is pomposity and hot air. Good old Huntington, there's a journalist on his way up, but sometimes he relies too much on his ability to ignore history. The "clash of civilizations" is the catch-phrase of the moment. Formerly known as the "war of religions," the concept has not gained any depth by being renamed. (For Braudel, who first coined the phrase, it had a different scope.) My colleague Huntington, with his simple ideas, seems to think the world began about 1000 C.E. He has succeeded (and the American label gives wide distribution to his writings) in transforming a truism obvious to most schoolchildren into a subject of planetary pontification. The first insight of his overview: the world is divided into different civilizations. What a discovery! But he forgot the catch: the world is also divided into nations, 189 of them at the last UN count. (The 188th was Palau, a Pacific island with 72,000 souls, and a lot of coprah; the 189th is the so-called Palestinian Authority.) Anyone with a practical sense knows that this is precisely the problem: cultures and political structures can only be understood together. Any discussion that neglects the latter is hot air. Chattering about facile, sophomoric notions such as the rise and decline of Western dominance, etc., is something within the reach of any manic-depressive. But it is another matter entirely to try to get a practical handle on that hazy, ill-defined, sublime verbiage known as the Occident. That insipid word nevertheless points to a set of values, and our best minds seem to have forgotten at what great cost those values were won and defended in the past. Whatever reality the word may still possess now, it owes to those struggles. In this respect, all civilizations are in the same boat. Can you imagine for one moment that there would be an Islam today without an Ummayad empire (only thirty years after the prophet Mohammed's death) and then an Abbasid empire? What would have become of Islam if Damascus and Baghdad had not been political capitals as well as religious capitals? And how many of the works of the great Sufi poet and mystic Ibn Arabi would have survived without the protection of Salim I, the conqueror who built his tomb and consecrated a mosque to him? Would Christianity exist today without a Christian empire, whether Byzantine or Carolingian, to halt the advances of the Arab cavalries? How could the holy monastery of Mount Athos have survived without the ramparts of Constantinople? Cistercian monks without the Frankish armies, the Jesuit order without Charles V..., the list goes on and on. How can anyone think that those three syllables "Wes-tern-World" are some kind of magic mantra that will ensure that the counter-attack is launched, or the treaty signed and enforced? Yet our opinion-makers seem quite content with no more than this mantra. Their casual invocations of words and deeds, their polemics, and their gestures are a never-ending source of amazement to me. They want the rose without the thorns. The pleasure principle is their only principle, which may explain their success at Rotary Club meetings. "Civilization" is a favorite word in their rhetoric, but "organization" is a trivial detail. Our loudmouths prefer hazy definitions.

Isn't it better to get your hands dirty than to have no hands? The big picture that some of us over here are quietly working out is a very demanding one, and it gets right down to the nitty-gritty. It will require a struggle to change our usual ways of seeing things, and of course that is harder to sell than a new currency. It will need a lot more than just a media campaign. We might even describe it pithily as a "revolution," but only in the strictest sense of a return: a movement around the circle, from fiction to reality. And what are the current fictions I'm talking about? In short, almost 200 micro-nations in an era of macro-realities. Their embassies, their intelligence agencies, and their surveillance satellites are growing and multiplying senselessly. The European Union, whether it's twelve or twenty-five, is also a fiction. So is the North America of three nations, and the Latin America of thirty. All this stuff is 19th-century mapmaking projected into the 21st! Do we really need to recognize the independence of all these Monacos and Liechtensteins when human destiny is at stake? Fiction and fantasy! What is real is the common destiny, and the growing vulnerability, of free societies. Let us put our international law experts to some truly productive work: transforming an integral space of meaning into an integral space of sovereignty. Let us answer the renewal of Islam with a renewal of democracy. Let us build the United States of the West by hitching our wagon to America's star. Let us recognize and use our real strengths. Our low population growth means that time is against us. The tide is rising, inexorably. Islam's strength lies in its shared fervor and its moral vigor; its weakness is in its political fragmentation into many states. Since Ataturk's revolution abolished the Caliphate in 1924, Islam has never had a political center recognized by all. With us, it's the reverse. We lack their moral and religious passion, but we have technology, and we also have a center. Let us transform our weakness into strength. Let us counter this world of appealing but fragmented, headless religious fervor with a democratic State with a real center. It will more than make up for the multiplicity of our convictions; and the boldness and swiftness of our actions will fascinate and paralyze our adversaries. America is a far more religious place than Europe. Faith is more contagious than doubt here, and its currents will move eastward across the Atlantic like the Gulf Stream. In the new, United Western World, our enthusiasm will infect you before your European defeatism has time to infect us. This may sound like the most ambitious undertaking in history, but it is not at all unrealistic. New challenges demand new responses. Our new communication and transportation technologies make this project feasible for the first time. You European intellectuals rightly bemoan the gap between our technological and political progress. Here is our chance to close that gap.

Islam is a religious community with no political cohesion. Let us answer its challenge with the exact reverse, since Christianity has long lost its power to unite our hearts. And let us put an end to the merely geographical division between the American continent and that exceptional extreme eastern extension of Asia. Its separation from us no longer makes sense. I don't have to give lessons to a media expert like yourself about how our global map is really defined by its vectors of influence. Every day, satellites and videoconferences abolish a little more of the old geography. The earth has shrunk by a factor of ten in one century. It doesn't take that much more time to cross the Atlantic than to go from the East to the West Coast. The time-zone difference from New York to Hawaii is just as great as from New York to Berlin. Twenty-first-century France is not significantly farther from the Hudson River than is California. Lack of land-links is no longer an argument. Otherwise Martinique would not be part of France, nor Alaska and Hawaii a part of the U.S. The 2nd-century Roman Empire stretched all the way from Baku on the Caspian, its easternmost military outpost, to Hadrian's Wall in England: over 3,000 miles on foot. It took at least a month to dispatch a legionary from Rome to the furthest borders. Can't we think at least this big in the Space Age? The Atlantic unites us, just as the Mediterranean did our predecessors. This Western Ocean is no more than a river running through our City, like the Seine through Paris. Does Paris need an *Hôtel de Ville* (City Hall) on the left bank as well as the right? Both banks vote for the same mayor. But as you know, Paris also has a remarkable system of *arrondissements:* semi-autonomous neighborhoods, each with its own mayor and local administration. In the same way, the nations of the future will have their own local governments. But Paris needs only one overall mayor, and why should we need more than one for our City of the Western World? A single geostrategic continuum doesn't need two heads. Future electronic voting via the Internet will become simpler, more secure, more transparent, and far easier to count, in our "Internation" of tomorrow. No more Florida-type scandals ...

And our future territory—how far will it extend? I say:

exactly as far as as the chill in our spines, which swept like a tidal wave through all communities of the Western World on September 11th. If we had a weather-map of that chill felt by television viewers around the world on that day, it would tell us far more than the pontifications of futurologists. Let us say that the island of our civilization—and the word applies, because a civilization must be circumscribed in order to be defended—brings together the totality of all the cities, villages, shacks, and mansions, where people of all classes, nationalities, and ethnic groups had a gut-feeling, an intimate recognition of America's enemy as their own. Start making pencil-dots of this on a map, and you'll end up with dotted outlines of this Island. It includes Israel, but not Palestine. Mexico is there, but not Chiapas. The northern shores of the Mediterranean, but not the southern. Perhaps Russia, but certainly not China. Perhaps Turkey (you know my fondness for Kemal Ataturk), but certainly not most of the Middle East, nor central Asia. And it's obvious that sub-Saharan Africa cannot be included. A richly ornamented Confederation: our Western World, to be defended. The word "friend" may sometimes seem meaningless, but never the word "enemy."

*

* *

And you French, what will you contribute tomorrow? A few spare boats for a patrol of the Gulf of Oman? A medical clinic on the Afghan border? Will you become a customer service representative for us? The more I read your Parisian press nowadays, the more I feel that France's national sin is a penchant for empty panegyrics. "Let us not give in to fear!" "The union of democratic nations must hold firm!" "Let us work alongside our American friends, and prepare for a long and bloody conflict." From *L'Humanité* to *Le Figaro*,[5] this surge of editorial unanimity does warm the heart, but if Western civilization cannot go beyond mere good intentions, then I wouldn't give much for its prospects of survival. Less poetry, please, and more logic! I am not doubting the sincerity of your ministers and editorialists, but I fear that your slogan, "We are all Americans today!" is more of a passing emotion than a well-thought-out position. By contrast, Kennedy's famous *"Ich bin ein Berliner!"* was more than just a humanitarian gush: it was also a strategic engagement. I grant you that there is a deeper and more welcome significance in *Le Monde's* surprising "We are all Americans!" than in that other, facile slogan, "We are all New Yorkers!" The latter sounds like a knee-jerk reflex of your long-haired

---

[5] *L'Humanité* is a Communist labor newspaper, *Le Figaro* is a conservative one.

adolescents, your old leftist hippies, or better yet, the visiting professor who comes to the Big Apple every fall to collect a nice Christmas bonus of dollars that he'll forget to declare on his French tax form. I agree that it's better to express solidarity with a whole culture than with a skyline, but even these sincere expressions have very low sustainability. To desire the consequences of what one desires: there's the real test. *Hic Rhodus, hic salta.*[6] There is no better touchstone for distinguishing bravado from bravery. Or for distinguishing the comedy of easy poses from the tragedy of hard decisions. Europeans clearly find it very difficult to let go of this shadow-puppet theater, silhouettes projected by a glorious past onto the screen of a trivial present. Only yesterday evening, I was sharing my thoughts on this with my old pal J.R., formerly a spokesperson at the State Department (the same friend who, against the formal advice of his department, intervened to unblock your visa when you were refused by Immigration because of certain of your more dubious connections).[7] He said, "The enemies of civilization want

---

[6] "Here is the Rhone; here is the leap." Attributed to Julius Caesar.

[7] An allusion to a personal incident of no importance. Upon arrival at the Boston airport in July, 1999, having being invited by Dartmouth College, I had my passport confiscated and was inter-

to divide us. We must be united in order to combat them." I asked him what exactly he meant by "united." When he resorted to the old saw of "alliance," I almost lost my patience. How much longer will we prattle on about the union of hearts, the spirit of Lafayette, independence within interdependence, our gratitude to America, and all those other lip-services at which you French excel? A little less goodwill, ladies and gentlemen, and a little more will! When will Europeans stop playing that old record of "our American friends," and "our total solidarity"? How much longer will you continue to be nitpickers? It is time to choose, once and for all, between your craven fascination with our power and helping us shoulder the burden; time to choose between the old subservience and the new citizenship. When we do win this war, it is my fervent hope that Europe will finally embrace the flag of the winner. And add its golden stars to the many more stars needed for the future. Each of us meeting the other halfway ... so to speak.

---

rogated for four hours (rather than the usual one-hour waiting time), even though French citizens are not supposed to need visas for the U.S. After a year of wrangling, and thanks both to Xavier de C***'s indirect intervention and to the persistence of the French Minister, they finally accorded me a limited "visa waiver" for "family reasons." These broad-minded officials had charged me with "uncontested collusion with terrorist organizations." [note by R.D.]

*

*   *

"Those who are not with us are against us," are the very pertinent words of my new President. And whether you like it or not, he's your new President too. For my part, I don't feel like a Fijian, a Tadjik, or an Australian. And I have no fondness for "working alongside"—my soul is not that of an auxiliary. How much longer will you persist in the illusion that those who decide for America are only beholden to voters inside its fifty states? The truth is, we are also deciding your fate. You are part of our overseas dominion. Is it fair, is it democratic, for us not to be answerable to those others whose future and field of action we decide? And we do decide it, whether you like it or not, and whether we like it or not. You never tire of speaking of a shared vision of the world, but how can that have any meaning, without sharing the sacrifices and trials of that vision? Certainly we all agree, Americans and Europeans, that it is a good thing to democratize the world's ignorant tyrannies, promote human rights, and revive the poorest economies. But how? A commonality of values that does not translate into a commonality of command is good material for after-dinner speeches, but no more. There are not two Occidents (playing first and second fiddle). There will be only one ... or none.

When it comes to running a modern economy, your left/right system has broken down. Even a god would have trouble distinguishing between a socialist finance minister and his right-wing counterpart. Why continue to separate ministries of the interior and of foreign affairs when it comes to organizing the defense of a single House? And what does it mean in practical terms, this notion of a United States of the West, led by America? My friend Jean-Marie Messier (I do hope his penthouse in New York was undamaged) is no more of a mincer of words than I, and he has been following this path by his merger of Vivendi into Universal. In my own small way, I have also done what is necessary so as to merge with the universal.

*

* *

You'd be way off-base to think I'm just betting on the winner. I'm neither an opportunist nor a supplicant. *Civis romanus sum?*[8] In today's world, that makes you more of a target than a superhero. In fact, it feels like my path has led me to the most exposed part of the battlefront, where most of the bullets are flying. My guess is that historians of the 23rd century will take the date of September 11, 2001, as

---

[8] "Am I a Roman citizen?"

the beginning of the end of the *pax Americana,* the turning
point of the curve. And my desire is to contribute toward
holding back the resulting tidal reflux. Over the years, I have
forged enough links within the "ruling class," and given
enough proof of my loyalty, to indicate that my present *xutz-
pah* is something more than just megalomanic ranting. You'd
not be far off to think of me as an old Athenian scholar,
imported by Roman power, haunting the corridors of the
Palatine, and occasionally taking an ignorant and foolish
Consul to task. What Derrida has done for literary studies
in American universities, I am trying to accomplish in strategic thinking among Washington's policy planning staff. And
not to deconstruct, but to merge and reconstruct. A bit of
historical *déjà vu,* no? Horace: "Captive Greece captured
her fierce conqueror, introducing the arts into the rustic
Latium." An exchange of civilities and full powers can
evolve into a true communion of souls—this was the case
during the century of the Roman Antonines, when it no
longer mattered where people's parents came from—as long
as the community goal of repelling the barbarian spears
takes precedence over the babble of native tongues. The
heavy Roman pyramid was easier to rebuild from the inside, as I know all too well. All the decision-makers in those
times were bilingual. Latin-speakers of the time of Cicero
and Juvenal had a solid Greek education, and anyone in

Caesar's circles who lacked it was considered a yokel. Things would be a lot easier for elitists like me, if our new Augustus, flying on Air Force One, made a habit of writing his intimate journal notes in French or German, like Marcus Aurelius, who took time between battles to write his *Reflections* in the language of Plato. In places like Dallas, the Bible seems to be the only book of wisdom in circulation. Not that I'm putting it down, but it's hardly sufficient. Cosmopolis America must be re-invented. The way things are now, our university libraries have amassed such incredible collections of the world's treasures of learning, that only a few crumbs seem to be left for the Capitol in D.C. The rare Kissingers and Brzyneskis blind us to the cloddish ignorance of some of the rustic senators on the Foreign Affairs Committee, where I have testified on occasion. One of these good old boys came up with this acronym: ROW, the Rest of the World. Very symptomatic! Nevertheless, isn't this robust naiveté, with its good intentions and its practical sense, its willingness to put its nose to the grindstone—isn't this better than the mean-spirited scheming of Europeans, rotten with their clever loopholes, spending all that energy in the search for a detour around the obstacle-course? François Mitterrand, your former boss and friend, was pretty good at this. Sometimes I wonder, at least momentarily, if I have really rid myself of my Frenchie complex—the complex that the Romans called *graeculus,* meaning a nitpicking little Greek pedant. The fear of such mockery (and the "de" in my family name certainly doesn't help matters) had some influence in my decision to clear my name once and for all. I speak American English, slurring and twanging my words like a true Yankee. But when I have a meeting with the honorable Senator from Kentucky, who made his fortune in farm machinery, I admit that Cicero's *Graecus homo ac levis*[9] passes through my mind. But at least with you, I can come out of the closet. Just between us Greco-Latins ...

*

* *

The debate on foreign affairs is going stronger than ever over here. A general soul-searching is in the air. There are even long, pontifical articles in the *Washington Post* and the *New York Times,* with titles such as: "Empire or Not? A Quiet Debate over U.S. Role," and "U.S. Urged to Embrace an Imperialist Role." You may have come across this sort of chitchat in the *Herald-Tribune* over there. If so, you will understand the magnitude of my task. These articles are a gauge of the level of awareness on this side of the water.

---

[9] "The Greek is flighty and inconsistent."

A strange "empire," indeed: horrified by its own shadow, like the rabbit in La Fontaine's fable, who leaped with alarm every time he saw the silhouette of his pointed ears. The old term "superpower" never really seemed adequate, either. And Védrine's[10] skillful epithet "hyperpower" seems to bother Puritan consciences. They want to see themselves as normal, and that prefix suggests some kind of pathology, like hypertension or hyperthyroidism. And "Empire" seems like an anachronism, as well as being incompatible with the Statue of Liberty. Evangelically incorrect. Sounds sort of monarchist, maybe even Fascist, and way out of the ballpark when it comes to freedom. These sensitive souls would do well to read Thucydides' *Peloponnesian Wars.* Athenians, who invented freedom for themselves, did not shrink from genocidal actions when, as leader of the pan-Hellenic alliance, they had to deal with outsiders, at Delos or Mitylene. Yet this did not prevent them from granting civil rights to those inside the *polis,* though of course slaves and non-Greeks were put on standby. And our hairy ancestors, the Gauls, finally wound up grateful for the comb and brush offered by their neighbor, Julius Caesar. In America, the very word *Empire* seems to evoke some sort of pathological indolence, a decadence like something out of Verlaine. That

---

[10] Hubert Védrine, a minister in the Jospin government.

old cliché, "decadence," has always hypnotized the pundits of the intellectual Left. Fortunately, John Doe doesn't seem to have this hang-up. In my view, it is the European who seems to be vulnerable to the dizziness of inward-looking. It's your Monsieur Dupont who stares at the great white barbarians on the march, and takes refuge in his crossword puzzles and whiny editorials. Over here, the energy is mounting, the flag is flying everywhere, and everyone wants to wrap themselves in the red, white, and blue. A renewal of pride, and a slap in the face to wake us up. So far so good— but I want my new national colors to become transnational. In my view, it is only by giving formal, official sanction to what is already the case that the ultimate nation will avoid the miserable fate of the later Empire. The history books never give an exact date, even in passing, for the end of the early/middle Empire. Was it the death of Commodus? Diocletian's rise to power? Constantine's conversion? The last scene of the movie *Gladiator?* The quality that is missing in Americanism is exactly the heritage that Europe failed to live up to: I mean the pride and daring it takes to be the New Rome, in one's own eyes and in the eyes of all, assuming that "to be Roman is to have a past classical model to be imitated, and a future barbarism to be subdued."

We must "de-program" our leaders about this whole question of Empire. They already have its capability, and its responsibilities, yet they haven't really grasped the opportunity it offers. You see, my wish is to serve as a pedagogue, via memos and papers (major articles in the press are more problematic because of my sensitive position, barring the use of a pseudonym). All those who truly know the past will be needed for this great work. Your half-educated contemporary scholars continue to make "empire" a synonym for sin. These demagogues confuse imperialistic pacification, which uses war in a systematic way to crush the weakest, with imperial politics, which builds and maintains the roads, makes the clocks run on time, and protects the weakest. The imperial "live and let live" is the lesser evil in managing conflicts between nations and among minorities. If you want convincing evidence of this, just look at what happened with the Eastern Empire, from Augustus Caesar, through Byzantium, to the Ottoman Empire. Need I remind you that the real end of the Rome of the Caesars came in 1923, when the modern Turkish republic was founded? The collapse of the grand, diverse Ottoman world into the shrunken, purist Turkish world culminated in ethnic purification, and forced migration of populations between Anatolia and Greece. It is nationalistic conformity that is alarming. There will be less slavish imitation of American culture in tomorrow's Empire of the West than there is in today's "independent" France, where the archetypal image of justice in the minds of youth comes from American-style TV trials. The Ottoman Empire welcomed the Jews who fled Spain during the *Reconquista*. And even Protestants received asylum from the Sultan (who went so far as to invite William Penn to build his first community on the shores of the Dardanelles — Pennsylvania almost became Turkish instead of American!). As late as the 19th century, it was better to have a name like Cohen in Istanbul and its empire than in any Arab country today. The multifarious faiths of that city remind us that the greatest moments of human civilization (no plural here) have coincided with an imperial organization. The latter is an open aggregate, the most effective form for dealing with cultural differences. All Empires die, as do all oak trees. But the golden fruits they yield are unlike anything ever produced by any nation-state. Empire is a fertile matrix that fits well with the pluralistic identity that we have now regained. Imperial retro turns out to be the authentic future of a present that is a polyphony of intermingling cultures. It is the structure that will enable the West to divide itself into as many subcultures as desired, without losing coherence. In any case, we no longer have the choice. In the last thirty years, the nation-state has gone through such a meltdown that it is no longer capable of dealing with NGOs like Al-Qaida, which have arrived to fill the vacuum, to say nothing of other uncharitable organizations, such as mafias, cartels, and cults. Since we cannot turn the clock back, we are compelled to move up to the next level. This ladder only goes up.

*

* *

"What we Americans of this generation and this era must accomplish is to truly become one nation," said Clinton in a state-of-the-union address, "What will we do? We are becoming more and more diverse. Do you believe that we can become one nation?" Talented, but immature, that aging adolescent. What he sees as a weakness is actually a strength, an order arising from disorder. What we need for the multitude of our inner voices is a pragmatic *modus vivendi.* You French are always complaining about a "unipolar" world, and you assume that a "multipolar" world would at least give you your sandbox where you could play in peace. But you overlook the possibility of a *unimultipolar* world, where opposites are brought into harmony. Militaristic order versus chaotic order: a false choice. The restructuring of this chaos, which has opened its arms to me, into an Empire that is conscious of itself would enable us to finally look unflinchingly at ourselves in the mirror. As long as we are afraid to appear as we are, we are not fully worthy of what we are. It is my conviction that Americans cannot

29

escape the charge of imperialism except by taking total responsibility for their imperiality. Empire demands that one become an arbiter, and not forever playing both judge and plaintiff, as in the Middle East. And the only way you reluctant mini-federalists will escape the status of a protectorate is by graduating from the status of second-class Americans to that of full Americans. Paradoxical? Good strategies always are. From financial markets to art markets, from Wall Street to Soho, from software to teddy-bears, there is only one country that leads the Western world. Why drag your feet and wind up at the end of the line, reduced to a parrot of the Voice of America? Like in those depressing, silly, imitative telethons of yours, where your pop singers raise funds for charity, singing *America, a Tribute to Heroes . . .*

*

* *

Instead of a true strategy, my well-intentioned, mechanical Empire has at present only a policy of pushing onward into the fog. World leader by chance, and irresistibly contagious. A power that is able to tame without coercion, using its two supreme, low-profile weapons: the dollar and the cinema, injected like a drug. Its hang-loose, easygoing style can only take it so far, and can even become a fault. If this de facto Empire does not mutate in the coming decades into a voluntary Empire, its chances of winning are about one in a hundred. I am betting on a win, because I believe it is capable of rising to the level of its destiny. Beginnings are always shortsighted and hesitant. The first Rome also took a long time to understand what was happening to it. Toqueville must have had an attack of historical myopia when he wrote, in *Democracy in America:* "I look back through the centuries, all the way back to the remotest antiquity, and can find nothing that resembles that which is here before my eyes." It's true that history doesn't serve up the same menu, but there is a lot more than a family resemblance between the pioneers of the Tiber and those of the Potomac, in their hesitant advances. A rough sketch of the family traits: prosaic pragmatism, a refusal of dogma, and a dislike of abstractions (Americans, like Romans, have little inclination for philosophy). The law, jurisprudence, and legal wrangling everywhere, from the doctor's office to the bedroom. An unshakable historical optimism, and a wholesome ineptitude for melancholy. A genius for logistics, a respect for engineers. A nouveau riche without false modesty, and a casual indifference to rankings of nobility among Greeks (or Europeans), the older culture's pride in its grand ancestors, divine genealogies, and ideals of tribal purity: contrast the Greek distaste for the *genus mixtum* with the Roman delight in its hybrid vigor. Uncle Sam also has little esteem for ancient lineages, preferring the value of what is new and young. Both imperial peoples find fulfillment in the conquest of space, rather than a fascination with the depths of time. Geography favors this, between the Atlantic and the Pacific. Our first Empire of the Middle—and I mean the West—took in most of Europe, a little of Africa, and a lot of Asia: the three regions of the known world at that time. The center lay on the median longitudes, with respect to the *oikoumenos* of that time. The same is true of our new *orbis romanus.* Just as Rome adopted the gods of her subject peoples, her reluctant heiress imports their cultures just as avidly, even to the point of instructing distant nations in their own history, draining their brains, and preserving their archives. Ancient Rome was xenophilic, and her successor opens her arms to foreigners from everywhere. And she knows how to make solid citizens of peoples from cultures with whom she has had previous conflict: second-generation Hispanics, Japanese, and Vietnamese make excellent patriots. Ethnic origin and language do not count. Isn't Colin Powell a Jamaican immigrant? And what about Condoleezza Rice, a child of Alabama segregationist society? The postmodern Imperium is trans-ethnic. It includes, not excludes. The earlier model admitted prominent Gauls into its Senate. Greeks, Iberians, and Celts wore togas and rose to high social status. And Marseille was allowed to preserve its Greek traditions in the federation. This is how any Empire worthy of the name goes about things, like a molecule bringing loose atoms together, giving body to the universal concrete. Instead of your lofty principles, pompously proclaimed, and promptly violated in practice, better to have customs that are respected without having to ponder them. New York City simply manifests human diversity, without having to indulge in vain philosophizing about it. Rome, the previous *Urbs Orbis,* was this kind of microcosm, with sedimentary layers brought from peoples everywhere, a confluence of statistics, maps, demographics, and roles from all over the civilized world. And just as Rome kept current registers of all its citizens, authorities are now working on a "universal identity" chip for every person on the planet, a computerized record of their skills, affinities, native language, physical characteristics, and even capacities.

"We Are the World," as the song goes. In this year of 2001, where else on the planet can anyone make such a statement without sounding silly? As Strabo wrote from Augustan Italy: "And now all the world is Roman. Some are called Umbrians, others Etruscans, Ligurians, Insubrians." Rome's successor might write: "And now all the world is American. Some are called Italians, others Mexicans, British, Dutch ..." To become American in the 21st century will be like becoming Roman in the 1st century. As my old fellow-student Claudia Moatti wrote in her admirable synthesis of current affairs, *La Raison de Rome:* to become a Roman "is to graduate from the status of Syrian, Spaniard, Gaul, or slave, to that of a man." Whether or not this past will enlighten our present, with the necessary and appropriate corrections, is strictly up to us, its amnesiac heirs. When it comes to territorial expansion, the famous historical acceleration factor has had only a moderate effect up to now. In those times, it took less than two centuries to move from the small Latium to the whole Italian peninsula. This is the same time it took for the United States to move across the continent and incorporate territory in Panama, Hawaii, and Alaska. Since then, things have moved much faster. Rome took twice the time to extend their Mediterranean sphere to the banks of the Euphrates and the Rhine, as we have to do the equivalent: the Rome of today would count its Eastern territories as Japan, and its Western as Australia. May we truly realize this destiny! Who but America can take responsibility, at a reasonable cost, for the peace and unity of the civilized world? Do you suppose we would breathe easier under the iron rule of Islam? Or under the domination of China, if by some misfortune she became the only hyperpower?

I would hope you remember your Roman history lessons—if not, dust off your old volumes of Piganiol and

Carcopino! Around 212 C.E., when the Goths grew too bold in the north, and the Sassanid Persians in the East, not to mention the Moors on the southern flanks, a perspicacious ruffian named Caracalla had the vision to grant full Roman citizenship to all free men in all the provinces. The only ones excluded were slaves and *deditices,* recently conquered peoples living within the provincial borders. This edict rejuvenated an exhausted Roman *polis* by bringing in millions of new recruits, with all their talents and taxability. This sudden generosity must have seemed scandalous at first, and I anticipate your observation that the edict did nothing to prevent the spread of Christianity (that troublesome, mushrooming religion, not unlike Islam today in Asia, Africa, and Europe). Granted, but this bracing emergency tonic at least staved off the barbarian depredations and the resulting Dark Ages for three more centuries. In any case, all our battles amount to no more than delaying tactics in the end, right?

If you are still wondering what my central point is (assuming that such a complex subject can have a central point), it's this: I believe the time has come for a new Edict of Caracalla—better thought-out than the original, and with all the alterations that democracy demands. You might object that the current reign of the opinion poll, which favors leaden feet and shortsighted policies (especially when amplified by

TV), would work against such a Herculean task as this. The first Rome, you may say, had the advantage of being governed by electoral arithmetic and periodic crises. Romans loved their sovereign without presuming to judge him (except of course for the tiny Senatorial caste with their sense of what was really going on behind the scenes). High politics worked best when no one talked politics outside of its designated space, in the sphere of the Palace. Rome had neither cafés, newspapers, nor general elections. I grant you that opinion is our cross to bear—but can it not be guided and shaped? Though things must proceed more slowly with us, the United States will have to accept sooner or later that they are no longer of America, but of the Western World. And those of the European Union must also agree to become federated states, having significant autonomy, but integrated into a single transatlantic union. A good small-scale analogy for this might be the status of Puerto Rico *(Estado libre asociado)* or of Quebec, a Canadian province that nevertheless has an international scope. There is no need to choose between local vitality and a larger collective dynamic. And you'd be wrong to dismiss this as utopian. We are already heading straight for it, the only question is when and how. For you Europeans, the sooner the better.

You detect a danger of extrapolation, of false analogy? True enough. But this only means that we must work *mutatis mutandi.*[11] Our elected leadership is a decent one by comparison. Son of the great Septimus Severus, Caracalla was a brute who had his own brother murdered, and ended his days by being stabbed himself. The only thing he knew well was making war. He ground down the Alemanns (now the Germans) and the Parths (now the Persians). He annexed Osrhoene, and pushed the borders of the Empire to the Tigris, in the heart of what is now Iraq. This bellicose churl nevertheless succeeded in taking the bull by the horns. You find Bush to be a bit of a yokel? Certainly no one would dream of according him a status, like the *Imperator,* above that of the common man. It's of no importance. The advantage of an Empire is that it is able to prosper with an idiot at its head. An Empire is also an intellectual commons that raises these idiots above themselves. The main difference in a democracy is that we no longer have to pretend not to see our Jupiters as clods with limited IQs, unworthy of religious veneration. All in all, a definite sign of progress. Democracy has its downside, but at least there are no assassins and rapists lurking in the corridors of the White House. Our elective Empire works by virtue of the function of the office, not the personality inhabiting it. So much the better for us. The President does his job, and his prestige (apart from the

---

[11] "Changing what needs changing."

occasional windfall of a charismatic leader, such as Lincoln, Roosevelt, or Kennedy) is derived from that office. The miracle of universal suffrage is that the most powerful person in the world can be a transparently simple-minded one. For complex minds, we have advisors, and they have always been recruited from the best universities and think-tanks. The elected *princeps* of the new Empire of the West, unlike their Majesties of old, does not have the burden of two bodies, the ordinary, mortal one, and the immortal one that survives him. These average folks occupy the summit, not by virtue of their character, but by the tools at their command. Truman was essentially a traveling salesman whose thumbs-down could decide the death, not of a bunch of professional gladiators ripping themselves apart for his amusement, but of 300,000 non-combatants on the other side of the world, in Hiroshima and Nagasaki. Technology amplifies to an extreme the eternal contrast between the personality of the decision-maker and the consequences of those decisions. And besides, the mediocrities who lurk in the corridors of power have never eclipsed that mysterious radiance of nations marked by the star of destiny. Think locally, act globally ... and never mind how things shift from one level to the other. When viewed from inside those corridors, all the Romes have their share of gossiping fools.

Incidentally, the paranoid fantasies of your anti-American

provincials over there truly make me want to laugh. If these naive blockheads only knew what a jumbled and confused mess really reigns in the secret basements of the Citadel! If they could only see how their thousand-tentacled, omniscient CIA monster, their conspiratorial White House, really operates! They would see how these all-powerful conspirators, hatching all their dirty schemes to get rid of opponents, are in fact jerked and pulled in all directions, at the mercy of the current mood in Congress, a Congress whose own actions are scattered and pulled one way and another by competing lobbies, obstinate subcommittees, and foot-dragging bureaucracies! Nothing is less Machiavellian than this big, clumsy Boy Scout. This supposed vampire of the world ponders one move at a time, forgetting the moves it made yesterday. To attribute fiendishly clever designs to it is to flatter it. The sad truth is, it only wants to do good for humanity—which, all things considered, is one of the best ways to do evil (and I personally can imagine the situation as even more perverse than this). You guys should stop attributing secret, long-term agendas to this manacled, floundering Gulliver, this pyromaniac firefighter. It is precisely a long-term agenda that it lacks, and that we need to help it find—and it will not be easy. What sort of Leviathan is it that was recently unable to subjugate three Somalian warlords, could not stop a Korean despot from making Bomb threats, and failed to restore calm to a Congo where it had already installed its own vassal? And was KO'd for twenty-four hours by a small group of programmed lunatics in search of a martyr's paradise? It is just this sort of improvisation that our combined mixture of virtues and faults should be able to squash. The American lion and the European fox together would make a wondrous beast—at last, the real, irresistible Janus Prince. A feeling for the common interest, for the general interest, and even for *l'espace public*[12] (English has no exact equivalent for this, and I doubt that Chinese or Russian does). Who could be a better PR man for this Janus than yours truly, a converted ex-Jacobin,[13] like a Spanish Jew maintaining the façade of a good Catholic (I ask you to keep that metaphor just between us). The Greeks had the gift of rhetoric, the Scythians were great goldsmiths, the Persians the best astronomers ... and the French are master-designers of new taxes and tariffs. Each to their own gifts.

Tu regere imperio populos, Romane, memento
Haec tibi erunt artes.[14]

---

[12] "Public space" (French). A rough equivalent might be the English notion of the commons.

[13] In this context, a radical Republican during the French revolution.

[14] "Remember, Roman, that it is yours to lead other peoples ... it is your special gift."

*
* *

The new international order that I'm outlining to you will require more than one change of borders, and we know that such a game needs two players. The more reluctant party risks being the stronger, because they believe they have more to lose. Let us count on time, our best ally, to uncloud their eyes. But let us keep our own counsel meanwhile, and waste no time preparing the ground. I grant you that the mediocrity of the electoral process is unlikely to bring a bold innovator into the White House, neither a Hadrian nor a Caracalla. It will fall to the Europeans to take the first step, by shaking up, mobilizing, and appealing to the bosses who run things over here. If the Oval Office should some day welcome one of your delegates, perhaps one of your commissioners, or rotating EU presidents, I have a clear notion of how this official, whether Belgian, Dutch, or Italian, should approach the Boss with this subject. The argument is quite simple. There are six main points. Here is my scenario of how this European leader might go about trying to pass some of the spark of his ancestors on to their current successor, the rootless leader of our common civilization:

1) Your superpower is far from overrated, Mr. President. But the tasks ahead of you are greater than your real powers. These are less than you may think, for they are constantly being drained by your permanent and growing responsibilities. Your "hard power" will be more and more circumvented from below, as exemplified by cutters on a jet plane and do-it-yourself anthrax. Your "soft power," your ability to get others to want what you want, will be circumvented from above, in space, by direct-broadcast satellites, which will diminish your powers of attracting and filtering. Your monopoly of world information is not eternal, and Al-Jazeera is an early warning sign. All things considered, do you really believe that your conventional forces and smart weapons will always give you the margin of superiority you need to conduct the famous two major conflicts, without having to take into account needs for pacification and police forces in places like Iraq or Yugoslavia? How much longer will it be feasible for you to fight through the intermediary of indigenous combatants, supported by air strikes from the safety of the skies? You are already over-extended. You cannot police the whole planet, from Indonesia to Panama, from Saudi Arabia to Korea. At present, you have a say in all significant military alliances. But what if the initiative were to pass elsewhere? For the moment, it is in China's interest to march in step with you (what government is not opposed to terrorism and armed subversion?). But if she decided tomorrow that it would be advantageous to make an alliance with hard-line Islam, whether Pakistani or Saudi,

Europe would soon panic, and rush toward appeasement (it wouldn't be the first time). Save our own skins, and never mind NATO and Article V. Fellow citizens will commit themselves, but allies drag their feet. You are not the only President who has to worry about opinion polls. Our politicians also know how to read the equations and draw their conclusions. Confucius + Allah = 70% of the planet's oil reserves and two-thirds of its population. Today, you are still a fascinating model, and are therefore loved and hated. But tomorrow? The balance of power is on the verge of a continental shift. Someday you will have to face this with your feet on the ground, ready to move. If your planetary mission still seems unclear, at least think of your own physical security.

2) You have yet to take full measure of the differential in demographic pressures between hostile foreigners with huge fertility rates and civilized countries with their families of one or two children. Have you ever walked in Calcutta, Istanbul, or Lagos? One person in two is under the age of twenty-one. The outlands are exploding, and Euro-America is imploding. In 1900, the West included one-third of the world's population, and dominated half of it, thanks to the colonial system and widespread illiteracy among indigenous peoples. In 2025, the Western World will comprise one-tenth of humanity, and now we are the ones facing the danger of illiteracy. You will be overwhelmed by Hispanics, as we will be by Arabs. And expertise in high technology will start to escape our control—half of all people in India and two-thirds in China have already become literate. Australia and New Zealand, with their ridiculously low population densities, will serve as spillways for overpopulation in Indonesia and elsewhere. The lands we control are shrinking rapidly: twenty years from now, they will pass from half to a quarter of the planetary land mass. This means that the armed forces of the least trustworthy countries, even the poorest ones, will become more and more dangerous. And those of the White-dominated countries, though certainly more professional, will suffer for lack of recruitment and enthusiasm. Cannon-fodder is running out, and what remains will consist of those with little inclination toward self-sacrifice, since the ancient pro patria mori[15] *has fallen into ridicule. Material prosperity will continue to anchor our way of life as long as your superior firepower enables you to pound the enemy from a safe distance, without exposing your boys too much, but nuclear proliferation will some day put an end to this. What better time than now, with the prairie crawling with hostile tribes, to begin putting all the wagons in a defensive circle?*

Your new immigrants, like ours, have a higher fertility rate. If we regroup ourselves into a single Federation, we can at least alleviate (if not overcome) our demographic morass by mingling one flux of immigrants with a different one. You have an excess of

---

[15] *Dulce et decorum est, pro patria mori:* "It is sweet and honorable to die for one's country."

Hispanics, and we have an excess of North Africans and Turks. The Spanish language and Latino interests are under-represented in a Europe with dominant Germanic and Anglo-Saxon peoples. This imbalance is to our detriment, because the Christian center of gravity is shifting toward the south. In 1939, the three most important Catholic countries were Germany, Italy, and France. Now, they are Mexico, Brazil, and the Philippines. You are closer to them. And we are closer to your enemies, and know them better. Your ideas are too simple for the complexity of Islam. You lack our proximity and our shared history (both positive and negative) with them. We always tend to demonize what we don't understand, and this explains the clumsiness of your counter-offensives, the confusion of your Middle-Eastern alliances, and the over-simplicity of your analyses. To the new Federation, you will bring your millions of Mexicans and other Latinos, and we will bring our millions of Moslems. The resulting combination will give us far more credibility as the world's leading voice. Our common State will be a true microcosm of the human mosaic, and a unequalled forum for intercultural dialogue.

The collateral advantage is huge, and essential: this revitalizing expansion will enable you to heal the ethnic fault-lines that you rightly fear, because otherwise they will soon be an out-of-control jigsaw puzzle. The integration of Europe will be like a return to the main roots of your history, as well as a revitalization of its WASP heritage. Need I remind you that your own census bureau

*predicts that your "non-Hispanic Whites" will comprise only 53%
of the U.S. population in 2050, with 25% Hispanics, 14% Blacks,
and 8% Asians? The addition of 300 million native Europeans
with Christian roots and light skin to the long list of children of
your Founding Fathers will have the effect of stabilizing your trou-
bled identity and correcting your path, preventing it from straying
from the values of those great minds. In the 19th century, 60 million Europeans immigrated to America. How many of us will you
need in the 21st, to reconstruct America? Only you can decide,
while keeping in mind this time-tested principle: the imperial soil
brings a thousand flowers to bloom, but too many will deplete it. A
nation falls apart when it becomes a fool's kingdom, where one
always has to work to figure out who is in charge.*

*3) The economy is not the main point of our argument, but it would
be hard to overestimate the superlative, exemplary economic effects
that the merging of our two traditions would have. Europe has too
much nationalization, America too much privatization. September
11th has taught you something about what privatized airport security leads to, as well as the sort of deregulation that offers air-traffic
controllers no job security, and as little as three months training,
which can lead to confusion between different airports. The old
model of state control is dead, but so is the neo-liberal model. The
cross-breeding of our practices and customs will put an end to the
absurdity of trade wars, such as surtaxes on foie gras in retaliation*

for bans on hormone-fed beef. Instead, we will unite and use each other's different approaches, discovering new solutions to our snarls, and corrections of our mistaken assumptions. Our old European superstition of the Welfare State will interact with your excessive reverence for market freedom, so as to create a flourishing middle ground, the fast lane of the future. For the good old days are gone, don't you agree? You had 49% of the gross world product in 1945, and only 23% today—a serious rollback. We have learned the hard way (in Latin countries especially) that you can't change the economy by decree; you have learned that you can't replace the common welfare with corporate culture. Our experience will provide you with discreet reminders of the importance of social dialogue, joint production committees, and employment policies. You will provide our subsidy fanatics with firm reminders of the need for mergers and downsizing. This new model will serve both the consumer and the quality of our products. Boeing and Lockheed will vie to acquire Dassault at the best price, and the superb research and development department that results will produce its Falcon *and* Rafale *aircraft for a better price. The French aeronautics industry, or what remains of it, will find plenty of advantages in this, as will your own. The ideal of tomorrow's Western World will include increased productivity* and *a better distribution of wealth. Mr. President, surely you don't believe you can achieve all of this alone?*

4) The issue of culture has become a daily battlefront for us in Europe. I realize this is not your main concern, and I shall be brief about it. You may know, in the current atmosphere of McDonald's versus Jihad, what a great alibi your movie industry provides for our own jealous filmmakers. Many Europeans, and some snobs in your own country, persist in seeing this super-industry of yours as a kind of inferior culture. It is in your own interest to disarm these critics, and to upgrade as much as possible this "Military-Industrial Entertainment Complex." This Moloch of celluloid, pixels, and terabytes causes misgivings in those who are attracted by it, as well as pleasure for those who love to complain about it. You've probably heard the accusations: cultural junk-food, the lowest common denominator, chewing gum for the eyes, etc. As your fellow-citizens, our whole-hearted contribution to this industry will give it a label of quality that will permanently silence the whiners and reactionaries. No longer will they be able to claim that globalization is just a word for Americanization (and in all honesty, it has sometimes been that). Hamburgers + Chateaubriand, soap-operas + Visconti, Coke + Rothschild, Disneyland + the Louvre, rock music + the Berlin Philharmonic . . . this addition of quantity plus quality will enable you to win people's hearts on two fronts: their pursuit of happiness and the raising of their spirits. Bluejeans along with Italian cuts, mass audiences along with the fine arts, huge budgets along with art-cinemas. Who would dare to rant anymore about cultural servility, stupidity, and conditioning? Our new common culture will no longer be equated with materialism and exhibition-ism, as yours is today in the minds of many Moslems. It will sim-ply be culture, with all its high and low points. Finally, the word will mean just what it says. "The sickness of the West is America," the curmudgeons say. Your reply will be: "The healing of the West is America." Alone, you are merely unavoidable. But together, we will be irreproachable. I might add that you will discover a new-found loyalty and enthusiasm for the Stars and Stripes among our artists and intellectuals, such as has rarely been found on your own campuses.

5) Such a mosaic of communities will require diversified laws, but you must guard against a weakening of federal institutions that would lead to a "Disunited States." Paradoxical though it may seem, the promotion of elites in your new outlying states will serve the cause of a strong central power, thanks to the influx of experts in regulative law (especially those with the Cartesian mind of the French) who are thoroughly versed in the machinery and pressures involved in a centralized State. These experienced loophole-closers will be able to greatly reduce the confusion, strengthening the exec-utive branch's ability to withstand excessive pressure from special interests. As matters stand today, you have ten times the influence on your foreign allies as you do on your own lobbies. This is not a healthy situation. We will help you to take back the reins, using our expertise in administrative law to create a central authority that comes across as more consistent, and as knowing what it wants. This brings up a worrisome subject: the current encroachments of your regional military commanders, the redoubtable CinC's,[16] on the prerogatives of your State Department officials, who have less money and means. When things go so far that diplomatic functions become virtually privatized, delegating assistance and development programs to NGOs and foundations, then it should come as no surprise that your generals are now nicknamed CinC's all over the world. Your State is no longer holding together. To illustrate with an analogy from the last years of Rome: you would be justified in fearing the progressive usurpation by your legionary chiefs, who pretend to be proconsuls, who are indifferent to the complaints of indignant colonials, as well as to the bitterness of local auxiliary troops. If things do not change, the CinCs will be fighting each

---

[16] Commanders-in-Chief. There are five regional CinCs, who divide up the world this way: The CinC in charge of the European command, who is also the Supreme Allied Commander of NATO, handles Europe, all of Russia, most of Africa, plus Turkey and Israel. The Central Command covers the new republics of Central Asia, all of the Middle East except Israel, and the band of Africa from Kenya to Egypt. The Pacific Command runs from India eastward through southern Asia to Hawaii. The Southern Command covers 32 nations of Latin America. A fifth region, the Northern Command, was recently created, and covers the American "homeland" plus Mexico and Canada.

other in a hundred years over the remnants of a dead Western Civilization. As President, you are Commander-in-Chief, but you control almost no troops on your own, at home. (This was also the case with the Imperator, in an Italy virtually without legions, an empty fortress whose natural defenders were elsewhere. He had to depend on the cooperation of the provincial armies in order to execute his decisions.) No doubt it will cost your skittish CinCs dearly to agree to abolish the distinction between U.S. forces and auxiliary foreign troops. They will have to hand over strategic commands to foreign generals who (with the exception of the British) they have been used to treating as flunkies. Already, your allies are balking at paying their military contributions in the absence of any political quid pro quo—after all, they have been executing orders without participating in the decisions. After integration, they will no longer hesitate, because their national interest will be the same as yours, and vice-versa. Just consider what your system of defense will gain from the exchange: new, enthusiastic recruits, motivated leaders, staff officers reinvigorated by direct contact with their real chiefs—totally loyal, and often "more royalist than the King." Instead of "playing an active role alongside the United States," as the hallowed cliché goes, they will finally be at the center—not just alongside, but inside, and in the front ranks. You might be tempted to wonder why you should pay for what you can already get for free. First, because command by hypnosis is never as effective as forthright, legal commitment. Second, the current "sharing of the burden" leaves you with far more than your share of it, and even your broad shoulders have their limits. With your new citizens, you will no longer "export" the costs of this immense military apparatus, spread out over 6,000 miles of territory, and already costing 40% of your federal budget, but simply distribute them. For the U.S. as it is constituted now, the time will come sooner or later (for Rome, it was the 3rd century C.E.) when domestic opinion rebels against the level of these expenditures as unendurable and fiscally unsound. If you don't act so as to increase the size of the taxable pie now, how will you argue in thirty years against the shortsighted and the fickle (and they are already numerous) who clamor to disengage from the ROW to save money? How will you survive a debate with the demagogues who claim that you are taking money from the poor in rich countries to give to the rich in poor countries? In giving citizenship to your oldest allies, you will be giving them responsibility. And you will silence for all time the sirens of isolationism, whether of the aggressive or the passive variety. You will also cushion the impact of any future recession (for the expansion of the 1990s must be regarded as an exception) by economies of scale and diversification. No more use for spies to ferret out secret economic data, when we all have the same balance of payments. The Echelon satellite will be put to better uses, as will all the industrial espionage technology—resources to use on our common enemies, instead of on each other!

6) And now, if you will allow me to anticipate your major misgiving, Mr. President: "America for Americans!" We cannot deny that your present citizens will lose some of their prerogatives. Historically, territorial expansion has always been paid for by a loss of privileges of some, and a denunciation of "outlanders" by the older populations. Aside from the possibility of some intermediate ad hoc association, let us take a good look at what is happening right now, before we start worrying about what might happen. Your own analysts are already saying that Israel is in effect the 51st state of the Union, Taiwan the 52nd, and even Turkey, in spite of its large population, is counted as the 53rd. There may be some complaints about this from the heartland, but they don't seem to be causing any serious problems. Have these de facto annexations weakened you in any way? Have they threatened your freedom? The legitimate protection of your democracy from a sudden influx of too many foreigners has always shaped your immigration policy. But what is a foreigner, really? There is no more difference between an American executive and his European counterpart than there is between a Democrat and a Republican. Whatever our social standing, in a time of crisis we will be Americans, first and foremost: citizens of the United States of the West. A long and well-designed educational campaign will surely mollify recalcitrants when they begin to see the advantages: justice without borders, new frontiers, America revitalized, the spirit of adventure and the pursuit of happiness reborn. We will be full partners in financing this campaign. Together, we will find ways to show even your most skeptical compatriots what dividends to expect from this huge influx of new funds to the federal budget. The doubling of the population and the expansion of American territory, like that of ancient Rome, will also expand America's glory and her sense of protective power. It will increase their sense of homeland security, by pushing potential enemies several steps further beyond a chain of buffer states. The Anglo-American common-law tradition will stretch from Gibraltar to the borders of Russia. It's true that this will not come without a cost: the expanded right to vote will naturally entail an expansion of the right to run for President. Forgive me if I seem pedantic, but I would like to point out that one of your greatest Roman predecessors, loved by his constituents and his troops, who vanquished the Parthian menace and extended the borders of the Empire to the Persian Gulf, was none other than Trajan, a Spaniard by birth. Septimus Severus, who spoke both Punic and Syriac, was of Tunisian origin; and Diocletian was a poor Dalmatian (or Croatian, as we would say today). Your great-grandchildren will elect presidents born in Mexico, Denmark, and even in France. But rest assured: they will be duly elected and sworn in only in Washington, D.C. (which was not always the case when emperors were elected by the legions, the elite Praetorian guards reserved for Italians). But in general, Rome was not always in the city of Rome. Under the Antonys, those famous voyagers, it happened more than once that the imperial staff and archives followed the Emperor in his travels. Marcus Aurelius ran the Empire from the banks of the Rhine and the Danube. And why not have a mobile State, one which can go on the road someday, if need be? Constantine went so far as to move his capital to the Bosporus, little more than an empty province at that time. It was a very shrewd decentralization maneuver, which put an end to the feeling and notion of encirclement. A center which can move to the circumference: this stroke of genius added a thousand years to the lifetime of the Empire, which was our original predecessor, the society most similar to our modern multicultural societies. The United States of the West, with a capital that can be moved to Honolulu or to Athens, or Ankara for that matter ... but let us not get ahead of ourselves. For the next century at least, we Europeans formally agree that Washington must remain on the Potomac. And any notion of equal sharing of power would be counter-productive. Double-headed eagles do poorly in gale-force winds, and we know all too well the consequences of two Caesars at the same time.

This is of course an excessively brief resume of the results of our study, a summary of our objective reasons, reflections, and prognoses. Mr. President, we of Europe now come before you, our honored and esteemed leader, with a petition for full rights of citizenship: not a green card, but a passport. You may well be tempted to shake your head in bafflement and dismay, but we beg you to reflect deeply on this. Our proposal is presented with the utmost seriousness and gravity. I leave you with this written edition of our study, which your advisors will want to go over with a fine-toothed comb. In six months, my successor will arrive to hear your response. Until then, my thanks for your attention, and my deepest respects to you, Mr. President.

*

* *

And now, just between us two Old Worlders! As go-betweens, our job will not be an easy one. We must persuade people to the right, to the left, and in all directions, often finding ourselves caught in the crossfire. Yes, but switching hats like that will do us a world of good! If I were lucky enough to be allowed to harangue a President of the European Commission, I would relish the task of persuading him to accelerate the process. Don't worry, I'd know how to use kid gloves with this exalted mediocrity. Other than the fact that your East Bank VIPs have notoriously thin skins, any radical dude who dares approach these guys with such a message must bear in mind that it will be better received if it is perceived as a plan to double the size of their property instead of a plan to demolish their house and build a new one. Personally, here is how I might tackle the job:

My dear Sir, you have nothing to worry about. You are only an executive agent, for this process is greater than any of us. What we are asking you to do amounts to little more than signing some papers—because the train is already building up speed. It started moving as far back as 1925, the year when Paul Valéry, who had an infallible sense for the hidden meanings of events, wrote: "It is clear that Europe aspires to be governed some day by an American commission." Ever since 1940, European nations have conceded the global dimension of their moral authority to America. But they will not start to really benefit from this concession until they openly accept the citizenship of the new leader—preferably before the year 2040. My dear Sir, don't give in to bewilderment! The two great currents of European public opinion which have done most since WWII to bring about European federation, representing both the Right and the Left, have always been the staunchest partisans of transatlanticism, and have supported every one of our agendas.[17]

---

[17]Xavier de C*** is no doubt alluding to the two great postwar partisan movements in Europe, often described as Social Democrats and Christian Democrats. These general tendencies have an approximately equal number of seats in the Strasbourg Assembly of the European Union. The least one might say is that they have never made any bones about their support for the fundamental foreign policy of our WWII liberators. We might add a third force to these two, more effective than they, because trans-partisan and trans-cultural, acting much like a digestive enzyme for the changes at hand: I refer to the so-called postmodern current. It claims to be on the leading edge of events—for it, anything that is not in some

The change we advocate is practically underway already. Language is the strongest creator of nationality, and nowadays you officials speak mostly in that language, whether at Summit meetings or in closed councils. Your own thoroughly French General Morillon spoke English while in Bosnia, and forget the fact that French is supposedly the other official language of the U.N. In your own eyes, as well as in signed treaties, the United States is a European power. With Canada, they chair the OSCE (the Organization for Security and Cooperation in Europe)—even more, they control it. Europe's only territorial defense structure is NATO. Open your eyes. All your fantasies of a fully European military counterforce have popped like bubbles, one after another. Does anyone today still speak of the Western European Union and its "security pacts"? Who still takes those musty European security fantasies seriously , like the OAEO, the FRUEO, the Franco-German Defense Council, etc., etc., generators of untold volumes of punctilious verbiage? Oh yes, and what about the much-touted "European Rapid Reaction Force"? What a clever catch-phrase that makes. Let's face it: all these things are nothing but wigs covering a bald head. They'll fly away in the first strong wind that comes along, especially when

---

way American-inspired is deemed to be old hat, retro-Frenchie, or even "Fascist." In France and elsewhere, this movement dominates editorial opinion and policies, and sets the norms for what is considered acceptable, interesting, or not worth considering. [R.D.]

it comes to funding significant movements of troops and supplies. The main function of these bureaucratic fantasies is to shore up your own faltering self-image. And there's no danger of that self-image overstepping its bounds: you have already handed the leadership of your Security and Defense on a platter to NATO's Secretary-General, a loyal U.S. subordinate. It is a good indication that you don't fool yourselves about the real nature of your situation. When the Berlin Wall went down in 1989, if you'd had any real self-confidence, you would have declared that the North Atlantic Treaty, a defense pact signed in 1949, when the Soviets blockaded Berlin, was no longer necessary. Outdated. But you preferred to hide your head in the sand. The upside of this is that by becoming fully integrated into the United States of the West, you will at last be in a position to demand from your "first among equals" full recognition and reciprocity. You will approach them as fragments of the true America in need, and desirous of joining the nation. Your candidature will prove to them the seriousness of your intentions.

European hearts have already been won by America, so the greatest part of the work is already accomplished. The rest is yet to come. In politics, those who do not build on dreams are building on sand. In the Old World, America is the dream, and Europe is totally invested in it. The European Union has no juridicial reality (it cannot sign international treaties, for example), because it is not an organization so much as an organization chart. Europe's institutional mystique is the method of one tiny step at a time, always waiting to see if others are following. This works when you need to move from the emotional to the judicial realm, in other words from below to above. Quid leges sine moribus?[18] *History does not progress by sudden mutations, it advances like a crab. The Edict of Caracalla itself was the outcome of a multitude of subtle, miniscule changes in customs. Citizenship had already been extended by the Emperor to army veterans, to Greek and Oriental luminaries and intellectuals, and to entire cities. Our equivalent process is also underway, and will continue. "Happy Birthday to You" has replaced all your home-grown birthday songs, just as Harry Potter has taken the place of the Little Prince, and Mickey that of our French Spirou (according to my grand-nephews at least). Americanization has already happened, and citizenship is simply the next logical step. It is like putting a roof on a house whose walls have already been built, but so gradually that we didn't notice the process, any more than we notice the growing of the grass. No transfer of sovereignty by ratified treaty will stand the test of time, unless it has been accompanied by a more instinctive transfer of loyalty: in a nourishment from images and music that reaches even to the level of physiology. For people only really defend something when they feel it as physically part of them. For European bodies, beginning*

---

[18] "What can laws accomplish without their corresponding customs?"

*with the youngest (things start to get more uncertain after the age
of fifty), the impact of physical experience is essentially American,
even (and especially) if the bodies happen to be Russian, Czech, or
Polish. The rock beat, the TV spot, McDonald's, popcorn at the
movies—from Charlie Chaplin to Clint Eastwood, from Miles
Davis to Madonna, our major identity models (as the psycholo-
gists say) come from across the Atlantic. The problem of "ideal versus appetite" has already been resolved. Your incorrigible intellectual
verbosity, your endless debates about "the architectures of power,"
so sophisticated as to be opaque, are a symptom that says it all:
your reflections may be European, but your reflexes are American.
And the former is powerless against the latter. Advisory committees can bring together the most brilliant minds, but if their proposals fail to strike any vein of popular feeling, they may as well
be cutting out paper dolls. On the other hand, when the vein is
already exposed, expert committees on administrative law can shape
and refine things. Their labors will not be in vain. The European
Parliament can always vote its nth regulation, and call for a referendum (with a 70% abstention rate) to "decide" the creation of a
European Federation of Nation-States (there's a nice square circle
for you). This intravenously fed dinosaur will be painted a demure
European blue (of a faded hue, with no blood-red to enliven it) and
the fluids that mostly keep it alive will consist of American sounds
and American images. There were a few of us who dreamed of
Europe as a world power, the one which would inherit the old*

French kingdom's historical mission of challenging the established world order. But this turned out to be no more than a pageant play put on by distressed orphans. And then one can always rationalize, like Jean Monnet,[19] and say: "If I could do it all over again, I would start with culture." Too late, Monsieur Monnet, Uncle Sam has already done it. And he went about it the right way. Acculturation; socialization; naturalization. This is the natural sequence in which a new State grows on fertile soil. Each season blends into the next, without upheaval. The unrealistic nature of European interventionism leads to an ungovernable mess, a view of political power that places jurisprudence ahead of music, milk production ahead of myths, and the euro ahead of the movie screen. The cart before the horse, the idea before the sensation, and the seasons in the wrong order.

In sum, your primary sin has been an excess of intellect. The European State has been the subject of a thousand complex and sophisticated speeches, conferences, analyses, and projects, but it will never leave the drawing boards. The Euro-American Federation, on the other hand, has not inflamed any speechwriters or media moguls, has given rise to no government reports, heated debates, forums, or talk shows. And yet it has already become a fact of your lives without being noticed. Mr. President, just take a moment to

---

[19] One of the earliest and most prominent advocates of the European Union.

consider what your average European would have to know about today, in order to be a good European citizen: to start with, a governmental structure with all the simplicity of a computer circuitboard: a Commission, a Council, a Parliament, a Court of Justice, Political Committees, dozens of community organizations, the seventeen obligatory procedures for making any decision, a list of forty unfamiliar acronyms and initials, and the latest update on compensatory payments. The good European should at least have a master's degree; the good American is just a cool guy or gal who watches TV, and follows the weather, the stock market, and the flag. American citizenship will allow your constituents to economize on their intellectual energy. No longer will they have to keep abreast of the latest monthly directives 94/95/XB/C32. It will greatly simplify their daily lives. Our true realities flow through channels that all begin, or converge, in places like New York and Los Angeles, not in Brussels and Frankfurt. "Europe, my own, my native land!" Can this be serious? A new money doesn't create a sense of belonging. I imagine your response: that the euro is now the daily pride of Europe—good, hard cash, the solid coin of the realm. But I suspect that it is really no more than a monetary convenience, a provisional measure to prepare you for the arrival of the dollar, the currency of your true future. I fail to see how a mere common currency alone can engender a true collective autonomy. Isn't this putting the cart before the horse? So you print your bills, and set up a multitude of monetary committees. But in all your cities, something else is being created much more naturally: your true civilization, your true beacons and points of reference. You know your stock exchanges follow Wall Street, your euro the dollar, your bankers Alan Greenspan, your scientific journals Nature *or* Science. *Your prime-time TV takes its cue from ours in America (reality shows are a good example), and your literary critics take theirs from the* New York Review of Books. *What real native originality is in your products, except for good cheeses, fine cuisine, and Hermès scarves? Your executive pace-setters, your new tools, are all derived from our culture. So are all your new catch-phrases: "the international community" (warmer, but less precise than your previous "the international system") or "governance" in place of "government," are only a couple of examples. Your buzzwords are all imported from the U.S., and you delightedly adopt each one, connotations and all. Your future leaders and managers are trained in our business schools, just as those from Thailand and Brazil are. As for your major presidential candidates, they know very well that nothing will give them credibility with their own TV-watching electorate like being filmed shaking hands with our Commander-in-Chief, or better yet, sitting with him before the fireplace in the White House, like old friends. The less lucky ones have to settle for Paul Newman, and failing that, a trip to Disneyland. What other country in the last fifteen centuries has been able to inspire a loyal following among youth all over the world, from the wealthy classes to the underclasses? We are all Americans, and we breathe this as we breathe the air—and this especially includes our anti-Americans, of the suburbs and the inner cities. Whether attractive or repulsive, the fascination is universal. Thomas Jefferson, the third President of the United States, and ambassador to Paris just after Benjamin Franklin, liked to say that for any civilized person, their first country must be their homeland, and their second country must be France. But now the formula has to be reversed. Today, the country that sent their GIs to liberate us in 1944 has become their first country for every young French, German, or Italian executive. We used to hear that Germany and France would be the two pillars of a new, growing (or maybe it's decaying?) Europe. But in fact, the little that these two great neighbors really know about each other is by way of those ideas, products, and works that have the American stamp of approval. And since fewer and fewer of the citizens of these two countries speak each other's language, they wind up having to speak the* lingua franca *of their unifying third party, a language which the French tend to disdain and the Germans tend to master. You may have noticed that there are no more direct intellectual exchanges of any significance between France and Germany, as there were in 1930. There are still plenty of communication lines, but they now pass through America, because it is there that our norms and standards are set: in law, in finance, in justice, in intelligence, and in beauty. Aside from gastronomy, the grades for originality, excellence, and good behavior are decided here, whether for your telephones, your films, or your governments. It's high time your whiners and wistful dreamers of "European difference" took a long walk down your own great boulevards. They will realize that their dreams have been trampled in the dirt, and not by marching Marine battalions, but by rollerblades. On my last trip to Paris, I happened to be passing through the* Place de la Bastille *about ten o'clock at night, and saw through my windshield the spirit of the times on parade. A vast procession of thousands of young rollerbladers were gliding in concentrated silence right down the center of the large boulevard, a fast-moving, compact, disciplined parade. They were accompanied by monitors, themselves on rollerblades, with "STAFF" marked in fluorescent colors on the backs of their shirts. This conquering army was escorted by a squadron of national police cars, to assure smooth and safe passage all the way across Paris. Most of these ecstatic, serious skaters had an image of the American flag on their t-shirts. A good sign: Americans are recognized everywhere by their pride in showing their national colors. Have you ever seen anyone from Hamburg, Seville, or Lyon moved to display a blue flag with a circle of gold stars on it—whether in celebration or in mourning? The average European has no pride in Europe, because their sense of pride lies elsewhere. Just ask these rollerblading yuppies if they need a special referendum to give them the right to pursue their happiness in this nocturnal glide once a week! It's useless to fight the inevitable: happiness may have been French in the 18th century, but it's American since the 20th. Your passport may say EU, but its libido says U.S. And so*

66

*does its compassion. As far back as our civic tradition goes, the pub-
lic moment of silence has always been reserved for national heroes
and martyrs. Did you know that for the first time in French history, it was dedicated to foreigners, in the recent nationwide observation of three minutes of silence for the victims of the September
11th attacks? This did not happen for Rwandans, Bosnians, or
Guatemalans. Does this surprise you? If so, it is because you have
become foreigners to yourselves, without knowing it. In reality, your
mourning has become imperial, just like your pleasures. And it
demanded this expression.*

*Let's skip the hand-wringing: there will always be plenty of dif-
ferent ways to be Euro-American. The principle of federated autonomy will play its full role. You need not relinquish any of your
local color. You say the death penalty has been abolished in Europe?
It also has in Wisconsin and in Iowa. The White House has nothing to say about it. Your home will still be your own. Every empire
is a mosaic of curious and contrasting customs. As for your careers,
nothing will really change. You might play second fiddle in Washington, or maybe even have a prominent seat on the Western Security Council (tomorrow's name for the NSC), but you will still be
number one in Essex, Burgundy, or Catalonia. The coexistence of
different States under a single Federation has never prevented healthy
competition on a local level. Better still: under such a Federation, a
de-politicized Europe will finally start to have real politics again.
In your present simulated union, real power lies in central banks,*

commissions, executive committees, etc., and it is not democratic. And the places where real democracy lives no longer have any real power. This is supposedly an enlightened despotism. But your so-called citizens elect Deputies, Senators, and Prime Ministers who have practically no handle on what is really happening. As a substitute, they produce communiqués—a form of diversion that soon wears thin. Your Lilliputian chieftains, elected by universal suffrage (in reality not so universal, because the poor abstain), gesticulate upon a stage with cardboard scenery. War, peace, legal standards, the politics of commerce, the great technological decisions, the budget, and the currency escape their control. No wonder they exude an aura of depression. By voting to elect the President of the United States of the West (the USW, or EUO in the French vernacular), integrated Europeans will finally have real influence on what is happening to them. Perhaps they will even rediscover a collective sense of their own manifest destiny. Wide-screen movies will be more effective than stained-glass windows in providing them with the mythic element necessary to anyone's diet—without it, people's souls die of cold. And for our solidarity, we must have the same national holidays for French, Germans, British—holidays which, for once, do not celebrate your neighbor's defeat.

Your elected representatives in the Senate and House of Representatives will either side with a clear majority or with a clear opposition—a reassuring cleavage that does not exist in your do-nothing committees, your halls of justice, nor in those mysterious regulatory commissions of yours, whose mandate and governance no one understands. You will be empowered to deliberate, censure, and choose. You will have more transparency and less corruption. And when need be, you will know better who to censure, and how. Your shakers and movers will have their say in all the newspapers that count, the ones that circulate in all major capitals (already the American Herald Tribune *is the single pan-European newspaper). You will have more access to real decision-makers, and your votes will weigh significantly on the scales. And you will see how the dissipation of your fog of ambiguities comes like a breath of fresh air. It will feel like finally finding the light switch after groping in the dark. No more of the waffling and wobbling malaise which I have perceived for years among my former colleagues working as diplomats, politicians, or military officers, hamstrung as they are by real constraints that they cannot reveal, and public-image dilemmas about unreal issues, such as whether to vote for Hardhead or Softhead. The building's foundation will finally support its structure, efficiency will support democracy. The end will come for all those absurd antics of simulation—the exit door from the theater of the absurd, found at last.*

In the meantime, don't be so quick to indulge in your favorite sport of railing against America's arrogance, unilateralism, and national egotism. You'll be only too happy to reap its benefits when the time comes. Luckily, there still exists a truly sovereign nation in this poor world! No one contests that sovereignty, least of all those Europeans who are always clamoring for real autonomy. America is an autonomous community. It bows to none, and follows its own will and its own interests. It was sheer fantasy to think that we could ever restrain, or halt this clumsy giant through international law and global structures, in the name of an imaginary collective security. Trans-national rhetoric only works within limits that harmonize with national interests and opportunities. The U.N. on our shores must become our instrument, or we will work around it. We don't need permission from the Security Council to bomb Iraq or Panama. Nor do we need the International Court to help us bring our pirates of the seas to justice. We make use of the U.N. when we need to, and don't come complaining to us about the lack of real democracy there! If there were, do you think you British and French would have permanent seats on the Security Council? What about India, to say nothing of Brazil and Germany? In 1996 the Security Council voted to re-elect Butros-Ghali as Secretary-General, by a majority of fourteen to one. That one opposing voice happened to be that of the United States. Two weeks later, our preferred candidate was elected instead. One against fourteen ... there was a skillful piece of work for you! As Pierre Schori, the Swedish delegate, told me, the main work of the 168 countries represented there is to maintain good relations with the 169th. Besides this, we measure the payment of our contributions to the U.N. according to the progress of the reforms in its operations that we "suggest" it undertake. You sigh that the current American administration does not honor its agreements, as with Kyoto, anti-personnel mines, sea-lanes, etc. Very well, complain if you like. But I wager you will not be so unhappy to have a strong helping hand, when the time comes, from the world's last country that can pass a federal law that nullifies a previous treaty. The U.S.A., by a stroke of luck, has managed to retain the power to carry out its own justice without the blessing of world opinion. Multilateral when we can, unilateral if we must. It all depends on you, whether or not our luck becomes yours as well in this State with one head and two arms—a State where your own nostalgics can at last satisfy their heroic quest. Only if it joins a unified West will Europe be able to really speak to the world, and better still, make itself heard.

Yes, America wants to give its European children a second chance. May Europeans (who never give a second chance to each other) take advantage of the opportunity! During the Cold War, Europe missed its own chance to shine. During a half-century of standoff between Eastern and Western blocs, ideological capitalism and hard-line Communism had real meanings. Not any longer. Our era no longer has a need for a De Gaulle-type mediator between two extremes. Also, the question as to which of your local politicians will be elected to preside over the nth convention charged with preparing the nth reform of European institutions is of interest to no one outside your vanity fair. What we lack at present is an ad hoc Committee to Coordinate Actions toward Western Unity. We need a coalition of elites, for once in tune with the mood in the streets, to help you extricate yourself from your Euro-federal morass, the last refuge of milquetoasts and cowards. At present you are part of the rim on the wheel of the West. Become spokes instead, and at least connect to the hub. You still dream of following your separate way? In the name of what? Show me one single value, one single ideal, praised by European orators, which America has not labored to put into practice. Peace? The last two World Wars were hatched in Europe, and it was America who restored peace. Much more recently, it was still Americans who had to intervene to stop the bloodshed among your Balkan tribes. Democracy? In America, even local judges and sheriffs are elected by the community. A more just distribution of income? Well, it's true that we see ourselves as more conservative than you in these matters. But when the pressure is on, we turn out to be more Keynesian than your Socialists. Your Central Bank eludes any democratic control, whereas our Federal Reserve must present an annual report to Congress. Giant financial interests have more freedom in Europe than they do here. Stop intoxicating yourselves with that moonshine called "the third way." There are now only two ways left: freedom and order; or servitude and chaos. It's our way or the other way. The choice is yours.

I must confess that the main advantage of these imaginary polemics is that I cannot be interrupted! In reality, I could well imagine our Brussels worthy kicking me out after a couple of minutes of this rant. And I can understand how his sort thinks. "So this is what you're bending my ear about—the *United States of the West!?* The grand adventure of a generation of Coke-drinkers and McDonald's-eaters? A half-century of walking the line, endless conferences, summit meetings, commissions, shouting matches, sleepless nights, referendums, vast tomes of reports, agonizing crises—and all of this, for peanuts? Not on your life." But all this man's labor is far from being in vain. His problem is that it has resulted in something quite different than what he expected and hoped for. But History always works so as to upset our expectations. Our most beautiful conceptions grow sour with age, and thumb their noses at us. In our own tiny lives, who of us has not built his or her own bridge over the river Kwai? For those who have been "building Europe," this perverse effect will for once be a salutary thing. It's not some Czar, or Mikado, who will be the winner in this game, it's the Genius of the West. For these myriads of righteous Christian Democrats, of whom I was one, the European Union will turn out to have been an indispensable prelude, a necessary mirage. Social psychology has its own rhythms, and these must not be jolted with a heavy-handed approach. We needed this transitional "denationalization period," like a decompression chamber for astronauts preparing to walk in space. Consider the example of France. Your old ideological leftists could never have made the transition to a more market-friendly philosophy, without the hope of paradise: a United States of Europe. And if my former colleagues of the Right had not worshiped at the same shrine, they would never have abandoned their cantankerous old notions summarized by the slogan, Work-Family-Fatherland. Without this decompression chamber, government contractors would never have given way so easily to pension funds, nor the SNCF[20] to the need to be more competitive. Previous to this, anti-Americanism, Communism, and the old Gaullist chimeras were too well-entrenched in our—I mean your—country. The potent elixir of social innovation must be drunk in small doses. This shows the value of myth, but it also shows the value of a daily exercise regime! All those countless Brussels conferences and consultations served as effective warm-ups, a training program in multilateralism, a half-open door to the new global reality. Without it, the average French citizen would never have come to accept the world as it really is. The European Union will have served well as a transitional object, a kind of security blanket. The Maastricht Treaty barely passed the referendum, so imagine how difficult a new Atlantic Charter would be without it! The language situation is a good indicator: every month,

---

[20] The French national railway authority.

ambassadorial coordination committees meet in each European capital, and those meetings are of course held in English. (By the way, they tell me that in Senegal the French ambassador still insists on French being spoken at all official functions, but that has the excuse of a local context.) The Finance committee would never have gotten the Quai d'Orsay[21] to swallow the pill (you know their priggishness in these matters) without the great rallying cry: European Power! The important thing is that in twenty years our rehabilitated government officials will at last be healthy bilinguals. French at home, English at the office. Serving the common good, without coming across as second-rate jerks. Now you see why I'm writing you in the future language of our workplace. I've always tried to get the jump on my peers.

Yes, I can imagine the bitter grimaces of the Brussels administrators, those worthy paper-shufflers who bend their backs with such devotion, making sure the show goes on. I would hope that when the hour of Federation comes, they will see the value of their work. Above all, Ladies and Gentlemen, don't give in to depression! Have no regrets! Granted, you've been plowing the sea—but your navigation has been flawless. Euroland, with its unshackled commerce and

---

[21] The French Foreign Office.

deregulated economy, is a solid and lasting achievement. Even better, it's a springboard. Your leaps have never taken you beyond the supermarket, but that's nothing to be ashamed of—no one is expected to do the impossible. When has anyone ever seen a State worthy of the name that was founded on mere consumer interests? How can there be a nation when there's no national army? A sense of homeland and belonging cannot be created by good management and trade. Like any true Federation, our United States of the West will be a whole that is greater than the sum of its parts, because its peoples' belief in it will make them willing to sacrifice themselves, if necessary, to defend it. The European Union remains a whole that is less than the sum of its parts. It has no sense of anything higher than the top of its own head, because it was born of and for nothing higher than comfort and good digestion. Its only forceful idea is a refusal of the use of force. It is *Emporium* rather than *Imperium,* discussion rather than decision. You are outmatched by America, and your lack of drive is not your fault. *Timor externus maxiumum concordiae vinculum.*[22] From the Battle of Poitiers[23]

---

[22] "Fear of the foreigner is the best means of creating harmony."

[23] The battle in 732 C.E., when Charles Martel defeated the Arab armies, putting a final end to their eastward advances out of Spain into France.

to Lépante[24] to West Berlin, over a span of thirteen centuries, Europe has never found a common destiny except while opposing a common enemy, whether the Moors, the Turks, or Stalin. Previously it was Rome who had to deal with Carthage, the Parths, and the Germans. As for those themes beloved of your speechwriters, such as "in the name of European values," or "being worthy of our dreams," it always turns out to be American G.I.s , arriving with their chaplains, rabbis, (and recently mullahs) who have to fix *your* problems. Without NATO, nothing would have been done to save Bosnia or Kosovo. Even in Macedonia, your soldiers needed their hands held in order to confiscate the firearms kindly surrendered by cooperative Albanians. Your citizens are deserting their churches, and aren't paying their generals. They've even done away with obligatory military service, which means that a continent of 350 million relatively wealthy and healthy people cannot muster 60,000 soldiers in an emergency, even for peacekeeping-type operations. As far back as 1940, French soldiers called it an "odd kind of war," where their task was not to fire, but to prevent firing from breaking out on either side. Apparently it was a piece of cake. My father told me how his batallion, on the Maginot Line, won a prize for the best flowers on

---

[24] An Austrian battle in 1571, when the Turks were turned back.

the front (there were three gardeners in his unit). It was already the Europe of Pétain.[25] How can you expect a consensus of resignation, a mishmash of second thoughts and reservations, to give birth to a vision and a strategy? Your jumble had some sort of substance to it when there were Soviet tanks on your eastern borders. Since the Berlin Wall went down, have you even been sure where your borders lie? Never mind the fantasy of Europe going it alone—how can you hope to overcome your internecine jealousies, your infighting, and stinginess, without a major threat forcing it upon you? How can your forget your old grudges against each other without the smell of common danger in the air? Here in Washington, D.C., since September 11th, Blacks and Whites now smile at each other on the street. They feel themselves as Americans, first and foremost. These days you can walk in the impoverished suburbs without fear. Every house is flying the flag. Cops and dealers joke with each other. In my neighborhood, muggings have stopped— my doorman can't get over it. It may not last long, but at least it will have served to remind us that fraternity needs adversity. In this light, your Europe comes across like an aged heiress counting her pennies in a shrill voice. If the sincerity of ambitions be judged by the means one commits

---

[25] The French administrator under Nazi occupation.

to them, then the members of the E.U. are telling a lot of lies. Its five major countries rarely give half as much of their Gross Domestic Product to defense as America does. Only Great Britain behaves with honor.[26] Primarily a commercial entity, the European Union has no honor, and therefore no soul. Its job is to make life easier for Europeans, and it dare not ask anyone to risk theirs. Like your new currency, it is little more than a commerce booster, and your Eurozone a trading zone, a dull knife good for spreading, but useless for cutting.

Forgive me for saying it, but this brings to mind the image of a guillotine—I confess to being a staunch partisan of capital punishment. How could you dream of having the guts to be a counterforce to America, when your own societies have lost the will to make the ultimate sacrifice, both outwardly (dealing with foreign aggressors) or inwardly (dealing with your own criminals)? How can you face death yourselves, if you are afraid to risk it? I don't deny that innocent people have gone to the electric chair in my adoptive country. Justice has its collateral damage. You see capital punishment as a vestige of barbarism. I see it as a symptom

---

[26] Britain's defense budget has been as high as 2.3% of the GDP, as compared to 1.77% for France. The U.S. contributes 2.87% of its GDP to defense. [R.D.]

of raw vitality, a sign that there is still a sense of the sacred here, a certain gift for sacrifice, and for irrevocable action. You Europeans are too complacent in your attitudes toward suffering, complaint, and compensation—as if compassion, a personal virtue, could ever be the foundation of a political system. In your public squares, and all along your boulevards, you have ceased to erect statues to combatants who have died for their country, or to the great who have served it. Instead, you erect memorials to victims: victims of massacres, of accidents, even of avalanches. Always ready to hear the cry of pain, and in dread of the battle-cry. Even your military officers have become social workers (and can you even tell the difference between these professions anymore?) I forget which of your Prime Ministers in the midst of an identity crisis said: "Europe is democracy plus social welfare." He might have added: "... and minus faith." American democracy lacks national health insurance, and that is not a good thing. But belief in God makes up for this shortcoming, by a hundredfold. Europe is America plus health insurance, but minus Providence. In other words, weaker psychic forces, less risk-taking, and more complaining. You have less taste for adventure, no taste for fighting, and some sort of state subsidy for everybody. "God helps those who help themselves;" or "Go on strike, the government will reimburse you." Which do you follow? Both slogans have their drawbacks, but I still prefer the American way of forging ahead with the first one to the European way of malingering with the second.

And to hell with those Eurocrats! They're grown-up enough to open their own eyes, and my powers of persuasion are limited. Get rid of the chaff, keep the grain. Have you looked closely at your new currency? The small coins are called "cents," which is a good omen for the euro-dollar of the future, but what is missing in these bills says more than all my prolonged rhetoric. Let's face it, they look like Monopoly bills: a feeling of some kind of no man's land, designed by an ad agency. On the front, a window (symbol of openness?). On the back, a bridge (symbol of good communication?). Five euros: an ancient bay and an aquaduct. Ten euros: a Roman portal and a stone bridge. And it doesn't get any better with 200 euros: a glass-windowed door and a viaduct. Not a single human being, not even a silhouette on the bridge, or under that archway suspended between heaven and earth, standing in a void. No portraits, no proverbs, no landscapes. Neither dates nor names. And you threw away your beautiful bills with Pascal, Delacroix, Debussy, and Saint-Exupéry for this continental play-money, with the look of a corporate stock certificate? When a friend at Crédit Lyonnais showed me some bills the other day, I thought of an opera scene, but with neither music nor singers. It's as boring as going out to vote for your E.U. delegates to the Strasbourg Assembly, which you are doing in ever-diminishing numbers.

Are Europeans to become a people without faces or beginnings? What about your heritage, what about your legends and fairy tales? OK, so you can't celebrate political and military heroes without offending someone else's national pride. But Erasmus, Newton, Darwin, Shakespeare, Goethe, Voltaire, Garibaldi, Cervantes . . . will you dissolve them all together in a soup, with a phrase like "Europe gives thanks to all its great men and women"? I understand it's not an easy choice: with 15 countries, soon 21, you'll have to deal with 21 galleries of great names. But when you reduce the mythology of a continent that has produced the world's richest mythologies to a few measly pictures of bridges and archways, one can only conclude that your offshore casino is anchorless and adrift!

The symbols on currency, or their absence, can be as revealing as Freudian slips. Yours is like a display in an artsy architect's catalog. Is this any way to get across a sense of a collective personality? The greenback has always displayed names of real people. One dollar: George Washington. Two dollars: Thomas Jefferson. Five dollars: Abraham Lincoln. Ten dollars: Alexander Hamilton. Twenty dollars: Andrew Jackson. Fifty dollars: Ulysses Grant. A legend is more meaningful than a treaty, and the proof is the durability of the greenback design. It speaks of the faith that America has always had in God and in itself, as it endured the two wars of Revolution and Secession. The hundred-dollar bill shows Benjamin Franklin on its face and Independence Hall on its back. This is money that encodes a memory unashamed of blood that had to be shed. Europeans would never imagine themselves as a chosen people—so much the worse for them. Europe is proud of its goat cheese and its paintings of old masters, but since it believes in nothing beyond good cuisine and cultural treasures, it will fall apart in the first gale-force wind. I prefer my one buck, with its beautiful array of potent symbols: Washington, the first Commander-in-Chief, with his powdered wig, the Eagle representing the Executive branch, the shield representing the Legislative, and the nine tailfeathers the Judiciary. In its right claw, an olive branch, in its left the spears of war. A good balance. And everything under the great Eye of the Divine above the pyramid, the Holy Spirit, eternally watchful. A good admonition. This paper rectangle carries a small lesson in heroism and the supernatural that anyone can read. It is also the emblem of a people who tend toward vulgarity and bad taste, I grant you that—but a people who has vitality to burn. It is the last messianic country remaining in our Christendom. The dollar has faith in the supernatural, and it is a currency of combat. The euro takes you into an architectural museum after hours. It was already old and aesthetic at birth. Hardly a symbol of destiny.

So let's not try to squeeze blood from turnips. The future breakdowns of your "European machine" can already be read in this pseudo-futuristic design, which lacks any significant event or deed worthy of celebration. A trust fund without trust, a stone tablet without writing. No heroes, no Churchills, no De Gaulles, not a shadow of independence to be found in it. Since when do a bunch of Central Bank directors and CEOs deserve the privilege of entering into the arena of world history without paying in blood, sweat, and tears? You've made quite a comeback since WWII, I agree—but greatness is not gained without passion, as the proverb says. Your Eurozone is little more than a trade zone, busying itself with milk quotas and fishing rights, unable to give birth to a real money or a real personality. For a long time, I too wanted to believe that a super-Europe could be the salvation of Europe. Alas, it's just more of the same, not a quantum leap, but a supermarket squared. Greater means, and less willpower. More member countries, and less capacity for decision-making. And why not jump on this bandwagon? Its demands are few, and you'll sleep better and save more money. As for the tribulations of the world outside Europe, let others take care of that. But this is an unsustainable cop-out in the long run. When ideas exude generosity and humanitarian feeling, it takes time to distinguish the true from the false. The false are praised from the beginning, but age badly. The true are widely ridiculed at first, but age over the years like the finest wine. So beware of ridiculing my Euro-American proposals too quickly. He who laughs first will not laugh last, nor best.

Good: so giving up the fantasy of Euroland isn't going to make you go into mourning. I suppose you can still console yourself with the greatness of your provincial heroes: Danton, Gambetta, Clemenceau, Mendès-France—the glorious roster! It's what you have to work with. And I know you can do better than this tiny list. National pride is a touchy subject, isn't it? But beware, my friend: the French have always had a talent for traveling first-class with a second-class ticket, but in the future the conductor will no longer look the other way. Your national vanity is a farce to everyone but you, "that fantastic pretense of the French to be leading a spiritual mission in the world," as Henry James put it many years ago, flabbergasted after a visit to Paris. Nowadays that feisty French ruffling of feathers recalls nothing so much as an irate old duchess, indignant at having to stand in line like everyone else. Let us be objective instead, and consider the reasons for abolishing France's permanent seat and veto in the U.N. Security Council. For one thing, why bother to maintain a right to veto that hasn't even been exercised in thirty years? If it's just a matter of saving face, we could imagine a special role for France and Great Britain in the United States of the West, a gesture of *noblesse oblige* (even in the old U.N., Byelorussia was accorded its own seat and nameplate right beside the USSR). No vacant embassies, that would be too heartbreaking. No, those ambassadorial palaces in Rome, Lisbon, London, etc., will only need a simple change of plaques: perhaps Agency, Representative, or General Delegation ... like Quebec, which maintains its own official agencies abroad, without being any less Canadian for that. In Paris, you have those regional agencies, such as the *Maison de Bretagne.* Why not a *Maison de France* in Washington, D.C.? It could even have a delegation chief, with ambassadorial rank. Some fat would have to be cut in the lower-echelon personnel, and an early retirement for the more obnoxious upper-echelon stuffed shirts—nothing catastrophic about that. Our venerable Quai d'Orsay will find a way to reconvert itself. Quebec, I remind you, has a Minister of International Relations with the status of a full government official, and even a chair at many summits and commissions. All the more reason to foresee such a status for France, at a higher level, and in phase with the progressive development of the U.S.W. Shared sovereignty will serve well as a transitional phase. Of Europe's Big Three, France will have the most to gain from this expansion. In the Brussels cauldron, it came out as the biggest loser of the three, in terms of relative weight and influence. That revered American ancestor and brilliant mentor, Great Britain, will actually have more to complain about than you, for it will lose its "special relationship," and will do everything it can to sabotage the integration. It will lose the special privileges that its common language and unquestioned loyalty now give it. No longer will it be envied as the only Athens for the new Rome. That role will at last be open for competition. As for Germany, its domineering tendencies and nostalgia for olden days of power will be largely neutralized. You will be less dominated by its leadership than you are now. For Europeans, the choice is between a Europe run from Berlin, or a Western World run from Washington. Weighing the comparative blessings that those two capitals have brought you over the last century, I would listen to the voice of prudence if I were you. What problem is there with regional autonomy when it is restructured and absorbed into a federation? Citizens of Louisiana have no reason to be jealous of Californians, even though California is five times as wealthy. One man, one vote. The U.S.W. will function as an equalizer of power, and put an end to all those petty disputes among you. Marianne[27] will get a face-lift,

---

[27] Marianne, a feminine icon, is the symbol of France.

and be cured of her chronic fatigue syndrome. And even better, because of her faithfulness to her vocation of philosophical trailblazer of progress, this somewhat derided prima donna will be the first to ask for the hand of the young lord as he is passing through a time of tribulation, thereby gaining recognition from both the future groom and the whole new family of in-laws. You have a trump card over all your neighbors: an intellectual elite whose stamp of approval carries the utmost credibility. I have no doubt that your leading-edge intellectuals will be able to give more *panache* to this opening toward the West, than toward all those countries of the East. No one is asking you to force the hand of destiny, nor to burn your bridges. But if France does not take the steps, both symbolic and juridicial, to show that she is smarter than her neighbors, and a step ahead of them in foreseeing the inevitable, she will find herself pushed back to third place in our indispensable alliances, far behind Great Britain and Germany, and perhaps even behind Italy. Those who truly understand their best interests can see beyond mere appearances.

What are the advantages? Today, the prime factor in a nation's world influence is to have an important diaspora at its command. The Armenians have one, but the Azeris do not: just compare how much foreign aid these rival neighbors receive. The Black Caucus was instrumental in changing

South Africa, and still looks after its interests, and the Jewish community has ensured Israel's survival. Black Americans protected Haiti, and forced an indifferent Establishment to oppose apartheid. But you French cannot hope for an analogous solidarity abroad. Americans of French ancestry carry less weight in the Senate allocation committees than do those of Armenian origin. Unlike Italians and Irish, you have no lobby to make your voice heard there. A bunch of restaurant owners, bankers, and professors cannot compete with the Greek, Polish, and Czech lobbies. Electoral lobbying, the most powerful of political levers, is even more closed to you than it is to the Germans and the Danish. You have no representation in Congress, and no entries into their decision-making process. Our French have not emigrated that much, and you won't make up for this by getting some Sophie Marceau-type beauty into bed with an important Senator, nor by hiring the services of a big Washington PR firm such as Ruder Fin, Inc. On the other hand, when there are sixty million French Americans, this handicap will be overcome, and you'll be playing on a level field.

To tell the truth, I wonder why I still mince words with you. When it comes to France, there seems to be some sort of odd restraint, some courtesy, some respectful indulgence from God knows where, which prevents people from being frank with the French about themselves. Let's start with that ancient mutual misunderstanding: Americans come to France with the impression they are not liked, yet they are; and French come to the U.S. with the impression they are liked, yet this is not the case. Americans don't give a damn about your changing moods. It's time your compatriots faced up to how small France has become in our eyes: the tenth wheel on the truck, and the one that squeaks and wobbles the most. And I doubt that the "friends of France" are really doing her a service by keeping their mouths respectfully shut about this.

Anyone who glances over a contemporary map of Nobel Prize winners, and compares it with maps of the past, can see that France is a has-been. Only when you leave it can you see how much it has shrunk. The voltage has dropped, like that sudden slump of energy of some people in their sixties—if you stay in the family, no one notices or talks about it, in the intimacy of stale old habits. I've been around too much over the last thirty years not to realize that France has lost its historical *raison d'être,* at least as a nation. The local culture still retains all its attraction, and tourists still love it. And yes, the sauvignon is exported, but the best Bordeaux stays at home, fine! Other than a certain sense of the good life, this country no longer has much to offer the world—it's too busy preserving circumflex accents, Roquefort cheese, beautiful alleys of plane-trees, fruits of past achievements, and nice retirement plans. Where is there any place for leadership in all this? Is it surprising to see the drop in attendance at your cultural centers abroad, or the elimination of your language from secondary-school curricula everywhere, in favor of English or Spanish?

Here's one example out of a hundred: did you know that for contemporary artists, French nationality means an automatic markdown of the price of their paintings on the world market? In New York the other day, I heard a well-known collector ask a gallery-owner from Soho the price of an installation by your famous G., so fashionable now in Paris. The answer was $40,000. "Impossible, I can't pay that much for a French artist. I can get something by an American or a German for the same price." It's the truth, check it out: in the list of the twenty highest-priced international artists, none of them reside any more in the country of Renoir and Picasso. Why do you think that French artists who want to make it big become residents or citizens here, to overcome the handicap? As for the art-lovers in your own country, they wax ecstatic about contemporary exhibitions at the Whitney in New York, or the Tate in London, but the very idea of an exhibition of contemporary French art in a Paris museum makes them blush with shame. The mysteries of colonial psychology ...

Of course this is pretty superficial stuff, I agree. More

significant is the simultaneous disappearance of great French theologians (Vatican academies have stopped including French as a working language) and great French military strategists. The ecclesiastical and the military are linked, as you know from history: the saber with the incense, right? My former defense ministry still maintains the custom of a delegation to the Department of Strategic Affairs, but what good is it, when others are thinking and deciding for you? What theologians do you have today to compare with the likes of Lubac, Congar, or Chenu? What generals to compare with Poirier, Gallois, or Ailleret? Paul VI and John XXIII were surrounded by French inspirers, both cleric and lay, but John Paul II has had to look elsewhere. And all your current leading lights in strategic studies piously translate what is happening at Rand, Brookings, the CSIS in Georgetown, and my own Heritage Foundation. I hardly bother to read what they write. Not one original idea since the "dissuasion of the stronger by the weaker" theory in 1960. The truth is that France no longer has a defense strategy of its own. You've simply copied our system of "projection of strength." And theological originality has passed to the Germans and Anglo-Saxons. In the D.C. metro area alone, there are fifteen think-tanks that are churning out real material. You don't even have one whose visit is worth a detour. Your *Collège Interarmées de Défense* still has a few Nigerians and

Comoro Islanders, but now even the Senegalese prefer to come directly to us. I suppose it's mainly because of the convenience of language that your own journalists who are looking for expert opinions on questions of security still go to your Foundations and Institutes, instead of directly to the U.S. Embassy. The only two countries in the Western World that still have a future are the United States and Israel. The first is on the ground, the second in people's hearts. For they each have a faith in their future. France has lost its future because it has lost faith in its star, and that European circle of stars is not going to restore it. You don't have to re-read *War and Peace* to realize how the great tides in the affairs of nations escapes the control of individual will. Napoleon himself was little more than a scarecrow in Tolstoy's eyes. This applies a hundredfold to all those third-rate politicians who have come to roost during the long calm after the storm of WWII. War raises the level, and too long a peace lowers it. Seen from afar, your stagnant fish-pond feels more and more painful to me. It's true that in those long-ago days when I worked in French Defense, we were anything but golden boys. But at least there was some kind of doctrine in those days. Since then, the only doctrine seems to be that of champagne and a flat tummy. Chevènement,[28]

---

[28] Jean-Pierre Chevènement, eminent French politician, known

the one exception to the rule, is an upright man. I got to observe him up close long ago, when I worked under your friend, General Henri Paris. You already know what I think of the Socialists, those didactic Pharisees. They combine the conformism of social climbers with the zeal of religious fanatics. But Chevènement, I must admit, cut through all that. He did his homework. Military staff couldn't sell him a bill of goods like they did the other political bosses that come and go. But you know how it is: one can respect the person without subscribing to his illusions. This is true in my case. And forgive me, but your "Che" set the bar too high.[29] That Don Quixote set his hopes on a France of dreams, of which your own Sancho Panzas have grown weary. Have you really realized that De Gaulle is dead? Not to mention Jaurès![30] The new electorate, and the young even more than the old, prefer the easy downward slopes, and

---

for his efforts to synthesize ideas of the Right and the Left. Minister of Defense in the 1980s and Minister of the Interior in the 1990s, both positions under Socialist governments.

[29] Régis Debray was famous in the 1960s for his friendship with Che Guevara, accompanying him as a journalist under dangerous conditions.

[30] Jean Jaurès, 1859–1914, statesman, philosopher, and founding father of French Socialism, assassinated by a nationalist fanatic in 1914.

no one is going to force them to climb back up! Granted, if France had any hope as a nation, it would be inspired by De Gaulle. For your sake, I'll leave that possibility open— we all need to dream. As for me, I've seen too much to believe anymore in such a rebirth. Your compatriots have lost their self-esteem. They have simply tiptoed out of history (no told them they had to leave), and now feel quite content about it. Who would dare to speak of wounded pride? They feel no pain at all.

I saw the proof of this a decade ago in the Gulf War, after the cease-fire. General Schwarzkopf, on instructions from Washington, informed us that the higher-ups would prefer that no French officers accompany him while the surrendering Iraqi delegation was being received. The British had a right to sit with the signers in the center of the tent, but not us. Our worthy General Roquejeoffre had to watch the formalities while standing in a far corner. Even though everyone knew that our TV evening news got its information from the afternoon edition of *Le Monde,* which got its from the morning *Herald Tribune.* Even so, I expected news of some sort of reaction from Paris to this slap in the face—an official government protest, a phone call from Mitterand to Bush Senior to put things right. Nothing happened. The humiliation passed like a letter in the mail. After all, what was there to be offended about? The time when De Gaulle could demand that his general sit at the table of the conquerors in Berlin has long been gone. I was among those attached to the Defense Ministry who disapproved of the Minister's resignation, just before the assault. But when I saw how we were treated when the dust had settled from the cyber-pounding in Iraq (and the distribution of juicy arms contracts in the aftermath), I realized that he was right, and I was wrong. But later on, when I saw how easily my (ex-)country swallowed these worms, with all its different elites in agreement for once, I ultimately reverted to my original position, but for different reasons. The times are too hard for captains who command no troops, however good their ideas. When would I, the diehard French revolutionary see that the game is over? The Republic! The Nation! The Cultural Exception! The European Counterforce! Why should I waste what life and valor I have left by chanting these catechisms, when the monks leading the chant are giggling under their hoods? Better to seek the ear of the Good Lord himself than that of his saints. You will see. In military matters, you will obey Britain, who obeys us. In all other matters, you will follow Germany, who follows us. And beware, for the role of third-string player quickly attracts a crowd. Not easy to stand out in all the commotion.

It has been my lot to have a front-row seat over three decades, with direct experience of every little move in the progressive slide down to abdication. Fresh out of the School of Oriental Languages, I arrived at the Quai d'Orsay early enough to know the days when France formally refused to accept orders from a NATO division commander, or be relegated to filling a gap in the NATO command. It was shortly after De Gaulle had been rebuffed in his demand for full equality with the U.S. and Britain in the tri-partitite NATO Command (no one laughed at the idea in those days). Much later, I lived through the period when France raised a hue and cry to demand a revolving NATO southern command (1996), though still leaving the 6th Fleet under the exclusive control of the CinC-Med. Three sneering rejections didn't dissuade her from rejoining the same structures of integrated command that she had resigned from in 1966. Nor did the recent fourth humiliation, where she apologized for having the impertinence to ask for a regional command. I remember the days when the Israeli-Palestinian problem was just about to be solved (or so our catechism told us) by a commission of the Big Four: the U.S., the U.S.S.R., Britain, and France. When this didn't materialize, we advocated that it be taken in hand by the larger structure of the United Nations. When that did not transpire, we found ourselves praising the U.S. for taking charge of the situation without all those distracting interferences. Finally, at the Conference of Madrid, I watched our ambassador lurking pathetically in the corridors, in hopes of buttonholing a staff-member he knew, who might clue him in as to what was going on behind the closed doors. National vanity, as I can testify, is a pernicious, but curable disease. (Just look how quickly Austria-Hungary vanished into smoke after 1918.) One gets used to anything, to being left with virtually nothing. And life goes on.

The sword is no longer the axis of the world, I agree. But in the most acute crises, it is still the threat of the sword that gets results, and not corporate cash-flow. Your nuclear sword (your conventional one too, though not nearly as serious politically) has been broken. This was done by you French yourselves, and done deliberately. For once, I was in agreement with your arguments, as outlined in your *Tous Azimuts.*[31] It's no accident that those ideas have caused no ripples (as you told me yourself, the book only sold a couple of hundred copies). You defended the importance of the Hades, the medium-range ballistic missile, the successor of the Pluton. You described it as a strategic missile, erroneously classified as tactical. Very well. So whatever became of your nuclear arsenal? To say nothing of your air force (Mirage IV + ASMP)? It vanished in a puff of smoke. Your forty Hades were recently cut to pieces with welding torches—

---

[31] By Régis Debray, published by Odile Jacobs, 1989. A book on geopolitical strategy and the North/South problem.

not even put in mothballs! Billions, gone with the sparks of the torches. No replacement for the strategy, and all of this in a general atmosphere of indifference. Your politicians, your experts, your weapons engineers, never made a peep about it. Your nuclear test sites in the Pacific have been destroyed—not even put on hold. Billions, sunk to the bottom of the ocean. Thirty years of colossal effort, to wind up along with the other small fry. And I suppose that all this leaves you indifferent, Honorable Sir, Secretary-General of the South Pacific Council? Never mind, I understand why— after all, tossing brand-new equipment overboard is an old national pastime with the French government. The magnificent, up-to-date *Royale* fleet of 1940 at least got to fire off a few salvos against Mussolini, before being scuttled forever. But now France wastes no time—arms are scuttled before anyone has a chance to use them. It's not capacity you French lack—you have plenty of that—it's will. Is unconditional unilateral disarmament supposed to be somehow related to human rights? You even went so far as to dismantle your production facilities for fissile material. The USA told you to sign the nuclear test ban treaty; and your Parliament ratified it, "so as to be in conformance with international law." That ban didn't impress the Israelis, the Pakistanis, or the Indians—they had more foresight than you. And of course the American Senate refused to ratify this same treaty (97 to 100), but you signed anyway, because you wanted to be nice. It was not unexpected. I tried to warn Matignon[32] long before this, but they just shrugged it off. Not one word of protest. And in fact, the American government was right to reject the treaty. Just because you tie your hands doesn't mean we should tie ours. The castration order applies to the harem eunuchs, not to the Caliph.

Was it resignation, or acceptance of reality? My colleagues over here have repeated it to me over and over, mincing no words: Why share decision-making power with people who no longer have the military means to back up the decisions? I recently learned that during the last NATO meeting, our delegation declined our European allies' offer of services. It was very nice of you all to offer your forces, but why should we wear a ball and chain? And have to give you a right of review in exchange? It's true that you French still have some communications, surveillance, and detection capabilities because of your space program. But if you want to play in the big leagues, you need more than two satellites. You are deficient in means of strategic command, as well as projection of strength. With your *Transall* program, you cannot even transport a military unit a couple of thousand miles. And in any case, your lack of on-site anti-missile

---

[32] The Hôtel Matignon is the French Prime Minister's office.

defenses would make it too dangerous if we left you to your-selves. You allowed the U.S. Air Force to repossess your Istres military base inside French territory. It was lucky they did, because your slow suicide was a painful thing to see. But you never cancel your programs openly, you draw the process out over time, allowing them to die slowly, for lack of funds, and especially for lack of courage. You postponed until 2007 the decision to build a twin aircraft-carrier to sup-port the *Charles-de-Gaulle*. But a single aircraft-carrier is almost useless. You took a quarter-century to put together a nuclear-powered aircraft-carrier, and it's still not fully seaworthy. Here, it takes six years between the decision and the maiden voy-age. Your Leclerc tank has no support vehicle, which makes it useless. Your *Rafale* fighter was supposed to be flying in squadrons eight years ago, but nothing's happened yet. Why did your politicians fail to take advantage of your advances in space, nuclear, and aeronautic technologies? In Afghanistan, it's lucky for you that our plans included a few secondary air-ports and land routes for your paratroopers to use (it's always good to have extra guards). But the most amazing thing (Wol-fowitz can't get over it) is how your Defense Minister goes to the trouble to take the train to Brussels to attend the Atlantic Council meetings, when he could just as well have sent an aide with a pen and paper to take notes. And all of that, just to get into the photo-op after the meeting! His calendar must not be very full. Whatever happened to self-respect?

Do you remember Herr Abetz's words when he arrived in Paris in 1940 with the Nazi occupation forces? "There are three powers in France: Communism, big banks, and the *Nouvelle Revue Française*."[33] Today, the Party has shrunken to a midget, the banks have capitulated to New York, and never mind the power of the press. What can be salvaged out of all this flotsam and jetsam? Preservation of the language of our fathers? No problem! Who doesn't cherish their own little peculiarities? We'd never begrudge you your badge of honor, that feather in your cap. Your attractive movies, with all their intimacy and local color, will be well-received. The same with your great fashion designers, your philosophers, and your critics. The French Academy (they might almost have invited you to grow to a ripe old age there, if you'd ever felt like fencing with them) will keep all its drums, swords, coats-of-arms, and esoteric lexicons. The best local traditions, all the pastry specialties of the realm, will be welcome in the U.S.W. of tomorrow: each province with its own picturesque quality. Our embassy in Turkey has already become a kind of proconsulate. But this doesn't prevent the Turks from fiercely protecting their own sphere

---

[33] A French periodical, whose tremendous influence waned after WWII.

of interests and cultural affinities. They even had the excellent idea of periodically convening a summit meeting of Turkish-speaking countries, including Turkmenistan, Uzbekistan, Azerbaijan, Kirghizistan, and Kazakhistan. You should take a leaf from their book—it would give more luster and class to those Francophone conferences and parleys of yours (alas, your commonwealth *is* poor in oil compared to theirs). No, but seriously: if you can exorcise the ghosts of Marx and De Gaulle once and for all, what fundamental objection could you possibly have to this proposal I am submitting for your sagacious consideration? It will be obvious, once you've gotten it. I needn't tell you that the positions taken by your big corporate lobby, the *Medef,* as well as those inside your French financial microcosm, give me reason to hope for the best. As for the elite of the corporate world, on the occasions when they have gotten wind of our "annexation" current of thought, reactions have ranged from calm to enthusiastic. One of my business friends went so far as to put it to a vote during a VIP banquet. Of the eight people sitting at his table, six voted for it, with delays. Only one vote against, and that was purely out of principle. And please spare me your populist sermons about the eternal treachery of the elite classes! That old leftist view has never shown any gift for prophecy that I can see. If it had really been in tune with the times, we'd all have joined the French Communist

Party by now—which would be neither very modern, nor very intelligent, as I'm sure you'll agree. Anyway, there's nothing to worry about. Our new Confederation's agenda will be so full, we'll find plenty of jobs to retrain the wobbling and the embittered. And as for your old friends with diehard leftist-nationalist convictions, they will be pleasantly surprised by the real benefits of integration. When they feel like railing against American government policies, your latter-day Asterix[34] critics will no longer have to go through the motions of pious preliminaries, bending over backwards to testify to their love for Elvis, Lincoln, and the GIs who died in Normandy: they can get right to the point of giving America a piece of their mind. No one accuses a French citizen who rails against his government of being a twisted "Francophobe." An Israeli who loathes Sharon is not labeled as an anti-Semite. In the future, you can launch all the salvos against Washington you please, from Paris, Madrid, Rome, or Prague. No longer will this be seen as a sign of knee-jerk anti-Americanism. On the contrary, it will be seen as a sign that you take your citizenship seriously. Colonized peoples have always loved to exaggerate. Your

---

[34] Asterix is a very popular French comic-book hero, a humorous symbol of stubborn Gauls, giving the Roman Empire a hard time.

French critics who routinely blame "the country of Bill Gates" for anything and everything that goes wrong will have to find another excuse, when that country includes everyone between the Danube and the Pacific. Your theorists who explain all evils as conspiracies hatched in America will have to find some other way to make themselves seem interesting. There will be a great rhetorical shift. Think deeply about it: for you personally, it's a win-win situation. Of course you'll have to abandon your romantic pose, along with your status as a deviant gadfly biting politically correct simpletons. But these losses will be compensated tenfold by the increase in your relevance, and the size of your audience. A naturalized "anti-imperialist" will become a dissident hero, a chic preserver of avant-garde values, respected and protected by the First Amendment, just like Mailer, Chomsky, Gore Vidal, or Susan Sontag. No longer a marginal eccentric. Everything to gain, right?

You see, the chagrin of loss is relative to the scale of things. When diluted in the vaster context of Empire, nostalgia will tend to evaporate naturally. A Frenchman who insists on keeping his nose buried in his tiny world of inspiration, mulling over his unions and strikes, may well become depressed. So will those Eurocrats who can't take off their blinders and give up their solemn gab-fests. The solution is to look at the bigger picture, with the sense of relativity offered by the long view. The miracle of the West will out-last "Europe," precisely because the torch is passed from hand to hand, coming from afar. Classical Greece was rein-carnated in Alexander's empire, and that Greece was reborn in the Latium. Rome was just another link in the chain, like America has been for Europe. In History, what matters is not those special human geographies where genius flowers and radiates for a century or two, but the movement that carries the flame from one oasis to another, from one elite to another. Islamic civilization was able to borrow nothing from its Byzantine predecessor, the Eastern Roman Empire, which lacked the flexibility of the Western Empire. The West had the gift of renewing and transplanting itself in fresh European soil. The Emperor Trajan was reborn in Constantine, who was reborn in Charlemagne, and onward through Frederick II and Napoleon. While sacking Rome, the Visigoths spared the churches and basilicas out of an instinctive respect. The spirit of our civilization is inextin-guishable, because it has always known how to renew itself without denying itself. It is the dynasty of the essential that matters, not the color of the flag. In my own way, I am finally discovering honor as a Roman!

So be it. My polemics have gone on too long. Forgive me the bombast. Seen within a vaster scale of time, the emergence of a new collective through the merger of two continents across an ocean (like Rome and Carthage?) is a sublime event. On the small scale, it won't be such a big deal. No doubt I could have spared you all these harangues if I had refrained from imagining fierce opposition; whereas in truth, most of our skateboarding European youth will feel only a sense of relief when the great moment comes. And all those potbellied officials in their marbled halls will jump at the chance to show how young and dynamic they still are. Your government honchos will learn discretion, with lighter, low-calorie protocols: no more VIP motorcycle escorts for their limousines, less fanfare and banners for their local functions. Let us be functional—and closer to ordinary people! An extra flag standing behind the official banquet table, the old national hymn still sung on local holidays, a simple reversal of order of those messages in French and English on Air France flights, and some new initials added to your passport. These slight rectifications in your outward signs of glory might almost pass unnoticed.

The handwriting is on the wall, old buddy. The first ones to read it will reap the rewards.

Have I been wrong in showing you the straight path, with no superfluous tangents and pirouettes?

See you later,

> your disloyal friend,
> Xavier

Epitaph

This has been a case of conscience. It was not without misgiving that I finally decided to bring to public attention (without much hope, given its current distractibility) a letter that seemed no more than a dark prophecy leavened by cheerful fantasy, until the tragic death of its author. Since then, it has taken on the resonance of the irreparable. After weighing my decision, I realized that it would be a disservice to the memory of my friend to respect his own letters PERSONAL, written large with a red marker at the top of the brown envelope. I could not allow it to molder in a drawer. I did my best to translate it faithfully, in my own way, for the first French edition. A guardian angel whispered to me that this long SOS was never meant to remain confidential.

Is my friend to be considered an Author? The pretentious connotations of that word would have made him laugh. A man of letters against his will, he had no ambitions in the world of contemporary literature, that vast cheese where every rat can chew a hole for itself. Nor was he at home in the world of politicians. He was a man of action, always preferring to be "on the ground," as they say nowadays. This letter is his raw confession. He lived in many worlds, was satisfied with none, and took mischievous pleasure in mixing fire and water. If he had ever settled into a single community, it would likely have been that of intelligence and marine infantry.

Our friendship—if that word applies to an unfinished argument stretching over thirty-five years—goes back to our university days of the '60s, years of champagne magnums and the rue d'Ulm.[35] Xavier de C*** arrived there during my last year. We were born to hate each other. I was on the far Left, he was on the other side: a Right without shrillness, and also without complexes. In that student milieu, he was swiftly condemned without trial as belonging to the wrong side: his name reeked of nobility, his hair was short, he attended mass every Sunday, and could run 100 meters in 12.9 seconds. His lean and lithe figure made him look like a military boarding-school graduate, though he actually came from a top lycée in the Latin Quarter. His haunts were the school corridors and libraries rather than the cafés. He had an absent, taciturn air, with his small round glasses perched on his nose, and his room with piles of books by Church Fathers from Tertullian to Augustine, in the

---

[35] A reference to the location of the Ecole Normale Supérieure, one of the most demanding and prestigious schools in Paris.

original Latin. His fellow Catholics, marooned along with him in this "red bastion," quickly promoted this athletic Latinist to the top ranks of the church-goers. His specialty was the Classical Empire. This left him with an annoying, lifelong penchant for Latin quotations, as we have seen here. One day I found a copy of his master's thesis on "The Parthian Opposition to Rome" that he had left for me. This was not a subject that I considered to be of any great importance at the time. Soon after this, to my great surprise, he suddenly walked into my room, in total violation of the sacred barrier that separated us — the good guys, the honorary proletarians — from them, the pariahs, the watchdogs of the bourgeoisie. But this sacrilege had the effect of breaking the ice between us. It was our first tête-à-tête. He questioned me in detail about guerrilla activity in Latin America (I had recently come back from there after a year and a half of travels). He also confided to me his doubts and perplexities as to the direction of his own future. Should he try for a place at the Collège de France? Harvard? A diplomatic career? Join a monastery? These wide vacillations revealed the rich and complex nature hidden behind the façade of an orderly, disciplined young man. This scholar obsessing over grammatical variations in the writings of Tacitus could also become passionate about the chaos threatening our former colonies. He was strongly tempted by all that sound and fury of a tale told by an idiot.... We continued meeting from time to time, always in private, until the summer vacation. His confidences made me realize how heavy the past can weigh on the son of an old and illustrious family. To make the burden heavier, my schoolmate was the son of a hero of the French Resistance. Even the strongest young shoulders tend to sag when given a model like that to follow. One of the earliest resistors of the Nazi occupation, his father had died recently of a sudden cancer of the pancreas, in his ancestral province of Sologne. He had been a cavalry officer who fled in 1940 to the unoccupied zones, where he organized clandestine arms depots. Betrayed by informers, and with the police at his heels, he managed to escape through Spain to join General Leclerc's forces in North Africa—but not before he had managed to sabotage and destroy large numbers of Nazi arms and artillery. Several times wounded, he joined the victorious liberation armies, and happened to be among the first group that arrived at the Führer's eagle's-nest. The grandfather had begun WWI as a simple lieutenant, and the vicissitudes of battle catapulted him to the rank of general, and the leadership of a regiment that held the strategic Aronde pass unaided. Yes, it was definitely a staunch, old French military lineage, but non-conformist enough to encourage the grandson to study Latin and Greek, instead of technology and administration. Xavier de C*** was a man of disciplined reserve, with the mind of a rebel. He was the opposite of our glib leftist slur, "Fascist," and had nothing about him of the braggart or the anachronistic crackpot. A Gaullist Republican,[36] warmed-over Vichyism[37] was hardly his cup of tea. Readers would be seriously mistaken to interpret his position as having anything to do with those fanatical Cold War crusaders for the "free world," obsessed by their absurd conspiracy theories and secret government betrayals. This tendency was especially active during the Algerian war, lurking on the margins of the Latin Quarter. Their shrill tones can still be detected occasionally in the voice of our new Right, modernist, market-worshipping, and feverishly "American" though it is. My iconoclastic friend was of an altogether different mold and different stock. It was for this reason that his change of citizenship seemed like a serious portent, and a grave warning—I can testify that when it came to forecasting the future, his predictions always hit the bull's eye, ten years in advance.

---

[36] In France this word has a slightly different nuance, evoking the ideals of the French Revolution and the Republic which emerged from it. "Republican" can apply to either the Right or the Left.

[37] Vichy was the seat of the collaborationist, sometimes Fascist, French administration under Nazi occupation.

Like many others who tired of the exalted trivia of scholarship, Xavier de C*** took his degree and opted for the National School of Administration. Actually, I was not all that surprised when someone told me he had gone over to *"Langues O"* (the School of Oriental Languages), dropping out of the college of Political Science in mid-term because he found the teachings in that national sanctuary of the common ground to be shallow, insipid, and conformist. This set him back several squares in the game of school prestige among those destined for important government positions. Compared to the keys to the Palace of the Republic, which his previous curriculum would have offered him, Oriental Languages was like getting in through the servants' entrance. For someone considered as "one of the most brilliant students of his generation," this sudden retreat, this donning of the modest mask of the hard-working specialist, was already a sign of his deviant path. When people deviate from the norm, they leave our field of vision—instead of worrying about them, we become indifferent. For many years I stopped inquiring as to what had become of him. No one, none of my old cronies even mentioned him that I can remember. This was strange in itself, in a small student milieu where, in spite of their divergent paths in life, people still liked to keep up with changes in the lives and careers of their old schoolmates—even faint signals that had been detected from afar, like a brief flashing of head-lights, were often reported over dinner in a bistro or a chance encounter on a Paris street. But there was nothing to be heard about Xavier de C***. No news of publications, no achievements, nothing. It was as if he had never been one of us.

That is why you could have knocked me over with a feather when I picked up the in-house phone at my office in the Elysée[38] one day, and recognized the metallic, syn-copated voice of my old schoolmate on the other end. François Mitterand had recently appointed me to a cabinet post, and my job was to deal with relations in "peripheral Third World trouble-spots" as they were rather conde-scendingly described even then. It turned out that Xavier was now working in Defense, as first adjutant to the office of General Studies, after a long spell with the General Sec-retary of Defense. The Republic had seen fit to recruit her son for his knowledge of Oriental languages, including some apparently obscure Turkish and Caucasian dialects. It was not long before we became confidants once again, in spite of our differences of opinion. My friend had not changed that much since our *Ecole Normale* days (and to tell the truth, nei-ther had I). There was one point of agreement that brought

---

[38] The executive offices of the French President.

us together: the need to defend public action against the growing winds and tides of a country where the market, the media-image, and self-hype had already begun to set the tone. Naturally he had heard of my misadventures,[39] and he shared his own in Asia with me—they were just as exotic as mine, and more instructive. Having learned Turkish at *Langues O,* he had moved to Istanbul in the early '70s, and worked at the Institute of Anatolian Studies, adjoining the ancient Palais de France, with a splendid view that took in the Bosphorus, as well as the minarets of Hagia Sophia and the Blue Mosque. In this old quarter of Beyoglu, he worked closely with his mentor, Georges Dumezil (who later gave his name to the Institute), and with whom he maintained a regular and stimulating correspondence, right up to the latter's death in 1986. (I would hope that some editor will someday see the value of publishing it.) That venerable scholar of Asiatic languages was known for having served for six years as head of the department of religious studies at the University of Istanbul, a chair that was specially created

---

[39] A reference to Régis Debray's years in Bolivia as a journalist and fellow-traveler with Che Guevara and his guerilla fighters. He was captured, tortured, and imprisoned. Only intervention from the highest levels of French society finally secured his release from prison.

for him by Mustafa Kemal. Like his mentor, and with the same disconcerting gift for mastering languages, Xavier's interests turned toward the cultures of the Caucasus. Traveling there, he became an initiate in the arcane tongues of Ossetian, Circassian, and Abkhaz. This traditional Catholic Christian married one of his students, a Turkish daughter of the Caucasian diaspora, fresh out of Galasgaray high school, and a passionate Moslem. "I'm more pro-Kemal than she is," he told me with a smile, "I'm the secular wing of our couple." This pure fruit of *tantum ergo* and holy water had somehow ripened into one of those rare Frenchmen who have a profound knowledge and love of modern Turkey—that Moslem country where women received the vote ten years before they did in France.

His expertise and his family name soon brought him important offers of recruitment from our military hierarchy. One might well suspect that this polyglot scholar, for whom central Asia had revealed its secrets, would have no great respect for military establishment bureaucrats. ("In peacetime," he once confided to me, "the Army is run by fools. Your promotion depends on your rating, and your rating depends on your immediate superior officer. The result? If you want to advance, you'd better hide your light. It means the boss is right, and the top boss is *always* right.") He finally found a compromise in an extra-hierarchical job, with one of those obscure entities with esoteric corporate logos, whose mission is to enrich the Army with new skills, outside contacts, and rational predictions—a kind of laboratory of ideas where independent thinking is not a sin. It has an approximately equal mix of career officers, technical experts, weapons engineers, and civil servants from the Quai d'Orsay. During my tenure at the Elysée, he coolly put my name on the official recipient list for copies of his classified notes and reports, soberly signed with his own initials (that semi-anonymity that was the administration rule in those days). These contained his analyses of situations on the ground, always brief (never more than three pages) and to the point. They enchanted me with their subtle, laconic mockery, their untimeliness, their intentional provocation, their total lack of that antiseptic treatment which produced the prudent circumlocutions of simulated neutrality that informed the usual "Ministerial Notes." Afghanistan was already a major subject, because of the Soviet invasion.

Chance would have it that the President, desiring more clarity about the situation, charged me in February, 1982, with the task of making contact with the leaders of the Afghan resistance, as well as with dictator-general Zia, the President of Pakistan at that time. I was supposed to determine what sort of aid France might offer, other than her good wishes. Mujahideen requests for military and material assistance were flooding the Elysée from all sides, from military to humanitarian agencies (there were bridges between them in those days), as well as from our celebrated pundits invited to the communion of the TV evening news. In that exalted atmosphere of anti-totalitarian combat, the Afghan freedom fighters, with their picturesque rolled turbans and baggy pants, had captured the zenith of our official imagination. But my old schoolmate was not seduced by the opportunism of the moment. He calmly pointed out the inconsequence and blindness of a solidarity that ignored the fierce, petty rivalries of that land. He despised the simplistic Afghan-cowboy legends that filled the newsstands at that time. Therefore, I received permission for my friend to accompany me on this mission. I had only to meet up with him in Karachi, where he was already working at the time. We spent several days together in the Northwest rebel areas, huddled with local leaders over military maps. Among them were several Pakistani military intelligence officers, including their future chief, the distressing General Hameed Gul (who ultimately resigned), as well as several warlords from rebel tribes. As long as I live, I will never forget the key moment of our journey: our meeting in Pakistan, in a suburb of Peshawar, with the cream of the Afghan resistance, gathered together for the occasion.

There was Gailani, the plump, perfumed royalist, seated

comfortably on a pile of carpets, signet ring on his finger. There was Gulbuddin Hekmatyar, the gaunt fundamentalist, face like a knife-blade, tiny recessed eyes, glacial regard. There was Rabbani, with his rolled headdress and his dogma on request. There was Modjaddedi, with kohl on his eyelids ... these are about all I remember in detail, but there were also several Tadjiki and Hazara tribal chieftains, whose names and even faces I've forgotten. Massoud was not present. It would have made a striking portrait, worthy of Bosch or Brueghel. Among all these feudal lords, the most progressive ideas came from the 17th century, as represented by the monarchist believer in the divine right of Kings. The most authentic of them was from the 11th century, and I doubt that he was inspired by the Arab-Andalucian enlightenment of that period. Such was my impression of the freedom fighters, the darlings of our raving intelligentsia: mountain brigands. Flabbergasted by the gulf between this glimpse of medieval times before my eyes, and the Afghan fantasy as seen from Paris, I took advantage of long translations to steal glances at Xavier de C***. He kept a constant, enigmatic smile on his face, throughout all the absurdities proffered by our eminent obscurantists. When the monologues were over, and the big and small chiefs had departed for their lands, their courts, their clans, or their mosques, I told him of my doubts: is it really necessary that we provide arms and support to these buccaneers? Do these turbaned anachronisms really represent the future? At least the Soviets opened schools, printed books, and unveiled women. Must we reverse all this in order to oppose their invasion? "Your questions are not the right ones," he replied. "Of *course* these guys are barbarians. If I had a daughter, I certainly wouldn't want her to marry one of them. Of *course* our media totally romanticize these ruffians. But it is precisely these medieval knights who will bring down the Soviet military machine. The Afghans don't know it, but the fate of "hostage Europe" is in their hands. It is our job to provide them with ground-to-air missiles and good military advice. Besides, if we don't do it, the Americans and the Saudis will. They're already in it up to their necks, and if we leave it all to them, they'll screw it up."

This was a strategy that looked at the long run, and knew how to distinguish between good intentions and their bad effects (a distinction ignored by terminal intellectuals). Xavier de C*** was a strategist, resolute and without illusions. He had intelligence, without the morose self-indulgence that so often accompanies it. In some warriors, faith inspires a kind of blissful cynicism: the ways of the Lord are mysterious, so let us be as twisted as He. But Xavier was different. Whenever anyone brought up values and ethics, my friend would reply: "With what force?" And if you spoke to him of the use of force, he would ask: "Out of what necessity, and toward what goal?" It's hard to imagine anyone less wishy-washy, and less accommodating. Xavier de C*** never forgot who he was or where he came from. He also never forgot the values that compelled him to oppose the same people he wished to help. He helped them for his own very precise reasons, and always in the context of an appropriately motivated strategy. Nothing was more foreign to this broadminded ethnologist than slogans like "We are all Afghans, we are all Cambodians, Bosnians, Moslems, Chechens, etc. . . ." Such slogans vary with the fashion of world events, and emanate from our weathervane ideologues, more concerned with their own image than with reality. Hysterical identification with victims is most often rooted in the fact that we don't really know them. We know neither their history nor their language . . . and above all, we do not know ourselves. This being said, we should not forget that those on the Right also have their "useful idiots," to use a term of the Bolsheviks of yesteryear. Following his recruitment by French intelligence to work in Afghanistan, my old university friend certainly never hesitated to make skillful use of generous but ignorant souls, privately chuckling at their vanity. Our secret services have no lack of discretionary funds, and have contacts in very surprising places. We know that they devote considerable time to communications and agit-prop. These days there exists a kind of leftist confusion that gives credence to every imaginable conspiratorial mishmash: our biggest undercover agent in Angola was obviously Jonas Savimbi himself, that black ally of the apartheid regime in South Africa. A champion of the free world like Xavier de C*** was certainly not unhappy about working in French military intelligence. The center located on Boulevard Mortier had been revamped, and it was there that he saw for himself the enormity of their means and audacity. Without going into excessive detail, let us simply note that the real adepts of media-manipulation, the impresarios of naive, simplistic, Manichean broadcasts and newspaper articles, the controllers who run those nauseating holy warriors and other useful idiots, take care to remain faceless themselves. When I teased him once about his penchant for keeping a low profile and covering his traces, he answered: "The puppeteer isn't supposed to be part of the show."

There is a problem about Xavier de C***. How is it that a far-seeing heavyweight like this could have remained in such total obscurity? His range of thought and action, his ease in moving from one world to another, and his inability to stay in the same place very long, are certainly traits that make him difficult to label. Was he a scholar? A secret agent? An adventurer? A strategist? His was a transverse personality that cuts through our categories and agendas. Those who provide good material for the legend-builders are supposed to wear a single hat—too much versatility is an obstacle. But what was he fleeing, by prowling in the shadows like a mischievous cat with nine lives? A burdensome father-image? And why do we French have so little reverence for our own trailblazers? Unlike Americans, we are lukewarm toward our true originals, including inventors and artists. Whatever passion the French have left seems to be reserved for athletes and pop stars, pre-packaged by the media and ready for consumption. Of course this calm rebel did little to invite popularity, with his talent for self-effacement, for offending important people with his fearless candor, and his deliberate tactlessness (and this in spite of his keen and very "politic" sense of subtle forces in relationships). He could be impertinent to the point of sarcasm, and a loner to the point of having his mail sent General Delivery. His dislike of routine often made him unpredictable. He was never a candidate for the Legion of Honor, which reminds me of a phrase from Barrès: "In this soul, revolted to the point of nihilism, honor stands upright and alone, like a castle in the Breton landscape." It seems impossible to determine whether there was more of masochism or of clairvoyance in the mixture that fueled this brilliant adept of Toynbee (and, I'm afraid, of Spengler). He admired powerful civilizations, and was obsessed by their signs of aging, their first colors of autumn. I cannot recall the name of the hypochondriac who wrote that "Success is an inevitable affliction, and the later the better." This melancholic man of action was painfully lucid, yet always ready to tackle something new. Taking action was his refuge from despair. I would like to believe that he followed his happiness to its conclusion. If he ever had the leisure to look back and ponder the choices he had made, I feel sure he would not have seen himself as a failure. However, like so many who travel in the shadows, he was not a man of influence in the strict sense of the word. He had too much insight and integrity to play the role of a grey eminence—that role requires the skillful use of sentimentality and obfuscation, which were totally foreign to his nature. We must learn to face the truth that our exhibitionist societies provoke aristocratic rebellion in some, who take pleasure and even pride in the opposite extreme of exclusivity and obscurity. Even today, there are a number of these to be found among civil servants—diplomats, jurists, military officers, and technical experts. In the years before WWII, Saint-John Perse (another Franco-American, who in those days was still Alexis Léger, Secretary-General of Foreign Affairs) offered this defense: "Let us keep this ring of Gyges[40] on our finger.

---

[40] A reference the story of the shepherd Gyges in Plato's Republic, whose ring gives him an invisibility which he misuses.

It is our consolation. But do not hope for any great merit in invisibility: you may well find more pride than modesty there." Our media-obsessed world tends to treat them with disdain, yet it is they who quietly stoke the fires of glory, just as psychotherapists quietly maintain mental health. Consider how important are the activities of the those unsung trainers, coaches, academic advisors, or those physicians and hospice workers who accompany famous cancer patients in their final moments, but whom no microphone or TV camera can ever seduce. Xavier de C*** was a sort of coach of anti-totalitarianism, and a hospice worker for terminal Superpower-Europe. A man who loved to work in an atmosphere of true mutual esteem, he was shocked to his core by the base degradation of public power he saw. His own reserve could not hide his pain at seeing the ancient, noble ideals of obligation and service degenerate into auctions of verbatim minutes of confidential meetings to the highest bidders, of directors of so-called "secret" services rushing into publication after retirement, and more recently, active leaders washing their dirty laundry in public, and in real time. It is my belief that this betrayal of the standards of ancient civic honor, whether of the soldier or the priest, had a significant role to play in his decision to leave the service of France, where the idea of serving without self-serving has become virtually forgotten. In his eyes, his masters had ceased to be worthy. He went elsewhere in search of that disinterested service, and joy in the gift of oneself—though we cannot rule out the possibility of self-flagellation, which is also an ancient national proclivity of ours. I would hope that a novelist would someday seize upon this destiny—it offers a story of paradox within paradox, worthy of a future Conrad.

The about-face of this patriot, switching horses in midstream, has something disconcerting about it, indeed. Is it just that he was an unconventional character with a need to devote himself to something vaster and more inclusive than his native country? His passion was self-effacement. This camouflaged marksman had no wish to be the hero leading the charge. Nor did he ever mount the podium as virtuoso soloist, preferring the anonymity of the orchestra pit. He was a Lawrence of Arabia in reverse, who would have chosen *both* the desert *and* the London office; and he would have opted for the Ottoman Empire over the picturesque Bedouins, in the name of a more exacting and global vision of the future of humanity. But now another image of him comes irresistibly to mind, one more in keeping with his obsession with Roman history: that of a reincarnated Flavius Josephus. This patrician of sound instincts was a Jewish military commander who switched to the Roman side when it became clear that the Jewish uprising was doomed. Long convinced that the Jewish fight for independence was a mistake, this learned and noble turncoat was fascinated by the formidable war machine of the masters of the world. He became the official prophet of the Emperor Vespasian, trying to convince his fellow Jews that "God has left our sanctuary, and is now on the side of those we are fighting against." The equally paradoxical Xavier de C*** doubtlessly felt the same way about us: stubborn clingers to a broken dream and a lost cause. If we were to reproach him for betraying the French ideal, he might answer: was it his fault that his country's moment of world glory had passed? The Genius of the West, perceiving the unworthiness of the old world, had crossed the Atlantic to the new—for him, this was sufficient reason to follow it, leaving no baggage or arms behind. It was for Europe's own salvation, for its very soul. The Jewish hard-liners branded Josephus as a traitor, but they were incapable of seeing that he really wanted to save Judaism, by helping it out of the blind alley it had taken. In his eyes, Roman domination was part of the divine plan—a disconcerting supernatural perspective. But the main difference between the two men is that Josephus spent his last days in comfort, re-writing the history of the Jews in Latin, an honored and pampered Palace hostage. But Xavier de C*** wrote in English so as to be logical and consistent with his position, not in order to

please his masters. He never gave up reading French literature, and was always interested in its points of style and
grammar. He was a mercenary of arms, perhaps, but not of
the mind. The proof is that he paid for his choice with his
own life.

In the early 1990s he was an attaché at the French
Embassy in Washington. Suddenly, and without explana-
tion, he requested an early retirement, which he obtained
two years later. Instead of returning to France, and an easy
life of well-paid administrative consultancies, he stayed in
Washington, where he was recruited as consultant for a
rather conservative foundation. It was after this that he began
to move up in the world of American strategic intelligence.
During our laconic correspondence in those years, he mentioned his green card to me with the childish pride of a
prankster, but said nothing about his project of becoming
a full American citizen. This was only revealed in the long
letter that I have published in these pages, the last one I
received from him.

In late 2001, he volunteered for Afghanistan, working
both as interpreter and as liaison agent between the DIA
post discreetly set up in Ashkabad, and a unit of Turkmen
fighters operating near the northwest border. His misfortune was that he spoke Turkish, and knew Turkmenistan
like the palm of his hand. His wife (from whom he was

separated) had family there, and was related to Niyazov, the country's President-for-life. This neutral desert enclave is approximately the size of France. It borders both the Caspian Sea and Afghanistan, the latter home to a million Turkmen residents. This was not the first time an American administration had used the services of this rare bird—he had worked on the project of planning underwater gas and oil pipelines to link Turkmenistan with Azerbaijan on the other side of the Caspian, and finally to the Turkish Mediterranean port of Ceyhan. For $2.5 billion, the U.S. could avoid having their oil and gas pass through Russian or Iranian territory. When the Pentagon asked him to return to the region after September 11th, he immediately accepted. It had nothing to do with bravado, nor hope of honor. It was because it was his cup of tea, and a job that needed to be done.

In the twilight of a freezing day in November, 2001, Xavier de C*** was killed by friendly fire, along with seven Turkmen fighters escorting his reconnaissance mission. They had encountered no resistance in their advance through the deserted slums outside Balkh (Bactrium to the Romans), a small town some thirty miles from the border, near the edge of the area scheduled for exploration. The explosion of a fragmentation bomb, dropped from an American plane that had mistaken its target, killed him along with a third of the escort, and interrupted radio contact between the group and its base.

Everything was done to play down any news of this tragic event. This is unsurprising in the context of a war of information, with secret plans at stake. The Talibans had little interest in this incident, even supposing they knew about it. The American propaganda machine obviously preferred it be forgotten, as did the French services, because of the potential embarrassment for them. Incidents involving such border tribes and auxiliary personnel carried a minimum risk of scandal. Best let the whole thing be forgotten.

The dismembered bodies were recovered the next day by the remaining Turkmen soldiers. This good Christian was buried by his estranged wife in a Moslem cemetery in Ashkabad, in the strictest family privacy.

Though my own part in these events is of no public interest (or rather, though I now feel so distant from them), I felt that this bitter misadventure deserved to be recounted—the story of this disinterested evangelist of Western civilization, obliterated by a misguided bomb from his new country of allegiance.

*

* *

My readers must forgive me if I do not respond, point by point, to the arguments proposed by my oracular expatriate friend. It is too soon ... or too late. I have no wish to upstage him, nor to rob him of the last word in this debate. Someday I will publish the correspondence that preceded this final missive. His widow has given me permission, on condition that his real name remains secret, because of possible repercussions in a family that harbors anti-Western sentiments. She also carried this name, and would now prefer it be forgotten. I cannot object to this. As far as she knows, he left no testament. As far as I know, he left no children.

My conviction that this letter should be made public is not only because Xavier de C*** perceived, long in advance, the key question of the century before us (once the illusion of Euro-euphoria has dissipated). It is also because these oracular meanderings resound with the echoes of a collapsing of foundations whose symptoms are everywhere to be seen. He had too keen a sense of humor to wish that this missive take on the dimensions of a manifesto, but I wonder if my indiscretion is not in accord with his real intentions, this lover of four-cushion billiard games. Xavier seems to have addressed, on a very high level (while reversing most of the value-signs), a widespread feeling of concern among us now: about the tendency to retreat to our tiny forts, our insidious desire to leave the slums of the world to their own fate, to sing in chorus with the Master, and to enjoy the coward's bliss of following in the footsteps of the powerful. There is no contradiction in refusing the American World Order, with its arrogance and ethnocentricity (however globalized in appearance), while still honoring the element of self-sacrifice to be found in the best of those Americans who are turning their backs on us old-fashioned republicans of Old Europe.

Is it necessary for me to point out, in agreement with our friend and adversary, that a united Europe could become something other than a syrupy collective anesthesia, if spirited men and women could bring it to recover its vanished taste for risk and effort? Democratic republicans regard the human race as a single people. They cannot condone the wall of indifference set up by a West forgetful of its debts in Africa, Latin America, and the Arab world, a wall that reduces these peoples to a vast sea of good-for-nothings, a sub-human mass to be managed, put to work, bombed, and brought to justice as we see fit. Islam is not our enemy, but our cousin in difficulty. We have a duty to help it find ways to adapt to a different era, as Christianity did (not without considerable pain) in the 19th century. As for France, it may have momentarily lost its way, but it has known other dark moments. Let us not darken the picture further—it is too early for a funeral ceremony. Finally, there is the ideal of the egalitarian Republic, still vital precisely because it is unrealized and incomplete. In a time when we see guard-towers of opulence and identity-ghettos springing up every-where, this ideal remains in our eyes as the most cheerful and enlivening of sins.

Whatever others may think, I am glad to honor the memory of an incorruptible man whose intransigence and insight left an indelible impression on everyone who crossed his path. This noble misfit will live in our memories as a violater of the rule that the giver of advice never has to suf-fer its consequences. A crusader, yes, but one whose deeds were in accord with his words. The ancient role of scribes has been to make the strong just, with no obligation to help make it come true. Hence it is not surprising that the hyper-Empire, at its apogee, can mold our brilliant minds and bring them under its wing. It is the task of others, isolated though they be, to make the just strong—working with modesty and perseverance, and disregarding the customary sneers and slurs. In France, there are still those who give priority to the task of resisting an overbearing power that nothing seems able to resist—a task undertaken by the all the Tintins[41] who still live in a Republic where vassalhood is not the order

---

[41] A reference, apparently both ironic and affectionate, to the French comic-book hero Tintin.

of the day. Better yet: in all our political melees, however dubious, a talent for thumbing one's nose at powers, thrones, and dominions remains the last gauge for distinguishing— with apologies to my late friend, and borrowing from his adopted language, which will never be my own—the *happy few* from the *unhappy crowd*.

R.D.

Born in 1940, Régis Debray graduated from the prestigious Ecole Normale Supérieure in Paris. He later obtained his PhD in philosophy. His early career was that of a journalist-adventurer. A leftist hero of the 1960s, his writings attracted the interest of Che Guevara, and he was invited to Cuba by Fidel Castro himself. He became friends with Che, and accompanied him as a writer and fellow-traveler during his guerilla operations in Bolivia. In 1967, Debray was arrested by Bolivian authorities while leaving the jungle. His claim to have been there only as a writer and journalist was rejected, and he was tortured and imprisoned. Che Guevara was killed later that year, and his guerrilla movement broken, but Debray remained in prison for three more years. He was only freed in 1970 after enormous diplomatic pressure was brought to bear, including pleas by Jean-Paul Sartre, Simone Signoret, Yves Montand, and even Charles de Gaulle.

Back in France, he completed advanced studies in philosophy, and wrote a number of books of essays and adventure. In the 1980s he was appointed to a cabinet post by newly-elected Socialist President Mitterrand.

For the last decade or more, Debray has become known as a leading "mediologist," and an advocate of overcoming the ideological dualism of Right vs. Left. In 2003, he was named by President Chirac (a conservative Gaullist) to head a special commission on problems of religious display in public schools, triggered by the national debate over whether girls should be allowed to wear the Moslem headscarf in school.

The Terra Nova Series

The Terra Nova Series comprises short texts by prominent twenty-first century authors exploring topics in the arts, cultural history, politics and international relations, and ethnic identity. The series is divided into:

American Narratives: Statements from the American experience addressing a global context; and

Global Perspectives: Texts by international writers addressing the boundaries and interplay among nations, peoples, ideologies, and cultural representations.

American Narratives

Brando Rides Alone
A Reconsideration of the Film *One-Eyed Jacks*
Barry Gifford
$10.95 paper, 1-55643-485-5, 112 pp.

The People's Democratic Platform
$10.95 paper, 1-55643-498-7, 80 pp.

Seven Pillars of Jewish Denial
Shekinah, Wagner, and the Politics of the Small
Kim Chernin
$11.95 paper, 1-55643-486-3, 112 pp.

Global Perspectives

The Geneva Accord
And Other Strategies for Healing
the Israeli-Palestinian Conflict
Rabbi Michael Lerner
$9.95 paper, 1-55643-537-1, 160 pp.

www.northatlanticbooks.com